AMERICAN HERITAGE
ILLUSTRATED HISTORY
OF THE UNITED STATES

The first responsibility of the federal work-relief projects, as this 1938 poster of the WPA maintains, was to rebuild the laborer's self-respect.

FRONT COVER: *The lonely desolation of the Great Depression is captured in a classic photograph of the Dust Bowl by Dorothea Lange.*
NATIONAL ARCHIVES

FRONT ENDSHEET: *A surplus of wheat meant low prices for farmers who, ironically, were further impoverished by the abundant yield of the American heartland during the Depression. These plains of plenty are shown in John Roger Cox's painting* Gray and Gold.
CLEVELAND MUSEUM OF ART, ASSOCIATED AMERICAN ARTISTS

CONTENTS PAGE: *Vanity Fair wryly recognizes the power of the New Deal's "brain trust," showing a mortarboarded NRA Blue Eagle abducting hapless Uncle Sam.*
COPYRIGHT 1934 CONDE NAST PUBLICATIONS

BACK ENDSHEET: *The Grand Coulee Dam in Washington, 4,300 feet long and 550 feet high, was begun by the federal government in 1933 and completed in 1941.*
JACK ZEHRT, SHOSTAL

BACK COVER: *Detail of a 1938 W.P.A. poster (top left), which maintains that the first responsibility of the federal work-relief projects was to rebuild the laborer's self-respect; Franklin D. Roosevelt (top right) suffered a fatal stroke as Elizabeth Shoumatoff was painting him; in the early thirties, hunger and poverty forced many Americans into breadlines—here, in the spring of 1933, a long line of people wait for free bread in New York City.*
NEW YORK PUBLIC LIBRARY; FRANKLIN D. ROOSEVELT LIBRARY; NEW YORK PUBLIC LIBRARY

AMERICAN HERITAGE ILLUSTRATED HISTORY OF THE UNITED STATES

VOLUME 14

THE ROOSEVELT ERA

LIBRARY EDITION
with Index in Volume 19

SILVER BURDETT PRESS, INC.

1989

Library of Congress Catalog Card Number: 89-50419
ISBN 0-382-09872-2 (Vol. 14)
ISBN 0-382-09878-1 (Set)

This 1989 revised edition is published and distributed by Silver Burdett Press, Inc., Prentice-Hall Building, Englewood Cliffs, NJ 07632 by arrangement with American Heritage, a division of Forbes, Inc.

Manufactured in the United States of America

AMERICAN HERITAGE
ILLUSTRATED HISTORY
OF THE UNITED STATES

VOLUME 14

THE ROOSEVELT ERA

BY ROBERT G. ATHEARN

Created in Association with the
Editors of AMERICAN HERITAGE

and for the updated edition
MEDIA PROJECTS INCORPORATED

CHOICE PUBLISHING, INC.
New York

Library of Congress Catalog Card Number: 87-73399
ISBN 0-945260-14-8
ISBN 0-945260-00-8

This 1988 edition is published and distributed by Choice Publishing, Inc., 53 Watermill Lane, Great Neck, NY 11021
by arrangement with American Heritage, a division of Forbes, Inc.

Manufactured in the United States of America
10 9 8 7 6 5 4 3

CONTENTS OF THE COMPLETE SERIES

Editor's Note to the Revised Edition
Introduction by ALLAN NEVINS
Main text by ROBERT G. ATHEARN

EACH VOLUME CONTAINS AN ENCYCLOPEDIC SECTION; MASTER INDEX IN VOLUME 18

CONTENTS OF VOLUME 14

VANITY FAIR

OCTOBER 1933 · PRICE 35 CENTS

CHAPTER 40

DEPRESSION AND A NEW DEAL

On October 24, 1929, the paper-thin prosperity that had dominated most of the '20s began a process of rapid, demoralizing disintegration as the stock market crash triggered a general economic retrenchment. All during the summer, stock prices had soared upward into the financial stratosphere, and none but the shrewdest had seen danger in the ascent. On the contrary, most buyers, intoxicated with the optimism of the times, thought every price gain marked the beginning of another speculative fortune. But, as seen afterward in the hindsight of bewildered analysts, September 3, 1929, marked a beginning not of fortunes but of failures. On that day, as the attention of many Americans was focused on Bobby Jones' progress toward the National Amateur Golf Championship, the Dow-Jones averages reached their peak. General Electric stood at 396 1/4 (on March 3, 1928, it was 128 3/4); United

The rich, bloated stock market of 1929 meets the virtual skeleton of its former self in 1933, in cutouts from newspaper stock tables, on the cover of Vanity Fair. *Sample shrinkage—Am. Power & Lt., from 156 to an emaciated 4 1/8.*

States Steel at 279 1/8, if stock splits and adjustments are taken into account (in March, 1928, it was 138 1/8); and Westinghouse's adjusted price was 313 (compared to 91 5/8 in March, 1928). After September 3, prices began to slip, recovered, and slid down again. During the week of October 23–29, they collapsed altogether. The rush to dispose of holdings became panic when those who were speculating on borrowed money had to sell out to cover their loans. Their fear spread; there was a wild scramble to get out from under. On October 24, about 13,000,000 shares were sold at sacrifice prices, many by brokers to protect themselves when their customers' margin of ownership was gone. The stock ticker fell so far behind that no one knew exactly what was happening. Whole blocks of stock were pushed on the market. Telephone lines were clogged; the trading floor of the New York Stock Exchange was in pandemonium. Despite efforts by Wall Street's biggest financiers, October 29 was worse; more than 16,000,000 shares were unloaded that day, the blackest in the history of the stock market. The entire financial world appeared to have come to an end.

The largest investors and speculators were the hardest hit at first, but thousands of smaller ones saw their savings disappear. Between the high of September 3 and a low on November 13, the price of 50 leading stocks was cut in half. Some $30,000,000,000 in capital values had vanished—a sum considerably above that of the national debt.

From Wall Street to Main Street

Americans had witnessed financial recessions before—some symptomatic of deep economic maladjustments and others merely surface disturbances. The most recent superficial one had been in 1921–22—a brief period of distress that gave way to the "seven fat years." Actually, these years had been more bloat than fat. A major segment of the economy—agriculture —had been in a poor state of health during the whole decade. During World War I, when crop prices were artificially high, farmers had extended themselves to buy more land, which they could not pay for when prices returned to old levels. Others had started to farm marginal land that was profitable only in an artificial price situation, and they, too, suffered when the decline set in. The administrations of Harding, Coolidge, and Hoover were well aware of agriculture's troubles and they all made efforts—large or small, sound or visionary—to alleviate them. But conditions worsened. At a special session of Congress in 1929, soon after his inauguration, Hoover had recommended the creation of what he called "a great instrumentality clothed with sufficient authority and resources to assist our farmers." These were bold words, suggesting a positive program. But the Agricultural Marketing Act of June, 1929, and the Federal Farm Board set up to administer it, remained largely untried.

Another cause of America's economic shakiness during the '20s was the increasing complexity of her industrial organization. Urbanization, a trend well established before World War I, shot ahead. The day of the commuter was at hand as municipal transportation systems and the rapidly growing number of automobiles made possible employment at greater distances from home. What had been cities grew into huge, sprawling urban areas—conglomerations of municipalities fused together. As the concentration of people grew, there was a mounting danger of serious economic dislocations. Business cycles showed a tendency to higher peaks and deeper valleys. The typical worker found himself more and more dependent upon the great industrial machine.

Efforts to save the ship

Herbert Hoover, shaken in the course of what had started out as a relatively placid Presidency, talked of recovery in optimistic terms. But less than a month after the stock market crash, he called together leaders of

In the spring of 1933, a long line, mostly of men, winds its way up to a small tent on a vacant lot in New York City to get handouts of free bread.

some of the most important industries in a confidential conference and asked their cooperation in combating the business slump. To minimize unemployment, he requested them to spread available work and wages among as many workers as possible. Two weeks later, he asked labor leaders not to demand further wage increases. Both sides complied for about two years.

Meanwhile, Hoover adhered generally to a policy of economic conservatism, determined to avoid government intervention, convinced that the deflation must run its full course before prosperity could return. His aging Secretary of the Treasury, Andrew Mellon, was so sure of improvement that he could say, on New Year's Day, 1930, "I see nothing in the present situation that is either menacing or warrants pessimism." By March, 1930, Hoover said he thought the "worst effects of the crash on unemployment will have been passed during the next 60 days." However, during the winter of 1930–31, the unemployed went over 4,000,000.

The President appointed an Emergency Committee for Unemployment

Relief to coordinate and advise on local efforts to solve the problem. He believed local responsibility and self-help were basic American policies with which he should not interfere. But by March, 1931, unemployment stood at 8,000,000—double the figure of the year before. Self-help was no longer enough—certainly not at the local level. Communities simply could not cope with a depression so all-inclusive. Cautiously the administration supported legislation for expanded public-works spending, which, however small compared to later programs, was at that time unprecedentedly large. Meanwhile, banks throughout the country were closing. By the end of the year, 1,300 had failed or had suspended operations.

Still clinging to his faith in self-help, Hoover called together some of the foremost financiers during the fall of 1931 and asked them to pool their resources in a credit reserve for some of their weaker associates. At first, the financiers suggested that this was properly a function of the federal government, but after some discussion, they agreed to try. The National Credit Association that resulted was a failure. It was followed by the Reconstruction Finance Corporation early in 1932, as the depression approached its most dismal depths. The RFC was chartered by Congress and empowered to loan around $2,000,000,000 to business. During its first year, it loaned about $1,500,000,000, but that did not make much of a dent in the depres-

A Baltimore man unsuccessfully tried this device to get a job in 1938, when the improving economy had a setback.

sion. About a month after the formation of the RFC, Congress enlarged the powers of the Federal Reserve System. By making government bonds and some other securities acceptable as collateral for Federal Reserve notes, the government released for industrial and business needs about $750,000,000 of the gold supply previously supporting the currency.

The people demand help

Hoover's attempts to solve major problems with cautious measures brought him increasing criticism. His

1178

WIDE WORLD

In the lean years, many of the unemployed peddled apples. Fred Bell, once almost a millionaire, tried it in San Francisco.

name had once signified thrift and saving—the "Hooverizing" of World War I days. But by the end of his term, it was associated with collections of shanties—"Hoovervilles"—housing unemployed, hungry people.

Administration critics held that the nation was faced by a crisis and that drastic action was necessary even at the risk of eroding personal initiative. As the election of 1932 drew closer, public opinion increased in support of this contention. Financial leaders had lost much of their reputation as sages and oracles. (Congres-

sional investigations were later to cast doubts even on the intentions of some of them.) The axiom "Business knows best" had more irony than authority. By now, the national income was less than half of the 1929 figure; unemployment had reached 12,000,000. One in every four workers was jobless. Cuts had reduced wages in the steel industry by 63% since 1929. Sawmill workers were getting as little as 5¢ an hour. Connecticut sweatshops were paying youngsters as little as 60¢ for a 55-hour week. Corn brought the lowest price since the Civil War.

In June, thousands of veterans poured into Washington to demand payment by Congress of an "adjusted compensation"—a bonus due them in 1945. They wanted it now, and by July, between 15,000 and 20,000 men had joined the "Bonus Expeditionary Force," living in improvised shantytown camps in and around the city while Congress debated a bonus bill. When the Senate voted the bill down, all but a few thousand of the veterans went home.

Other events over which he had little control combined to plague the unhappy engineer in the White House. During the summer of 1931, the European economic situation deteriorated badly. The Kreditanstalt, Austria's most influential bank, got into serious difficulties, and the Austrian government's frantic attempts to save it spread fear throughout Europe. Hoover recognized the dangers of the

1179

Fatally wounded, Mayor Anton Cermak of Chicago is helped to a car after being hit by a bullet meant for President-elect Roosevelt in Miami, February 15, 1933.

situation and proposed a year's moratorium on war debts and reparation payments to ease the strain on the other side of the Atlantic. (Few countries were keeping up their payments, anyway.) It was not enough. Before long, German financial houses were in trouble. Then difficulties arose among British institutions. On September 21, 1931, England abandoned the gold standard—a move that drove down the prices of foreign investments on the New York Stock Exchange and in turn affected American banking firms. A new wave of hoarding resulted.

Mandate for a new deal

The Democrats had not elected a President since 1916, but they were confident that 1932 was to be their year. Many of them favored New York's progressive governor, Franklin Delano Roosevelt. He had served as Assistant Secretary of the Navy and was the Democrats' nominee for Vice-President in 1920. In the 1928 election, when Alfred E. Smith had lost New York by 100,000 votes, Roosevelt had moved into the state capitol at Albany with a plurality of 25,000. In the 1930 election, he was returned to the governorship by a plurality of 725,000, a record for New York.

Roosevelt had nationally known rivals in John Nance Garner, Speaker of the House, and Al Smith. But the battle for the nomination was brief. With a majority on the first ballot, Roosevelt was able to get the necessary two-thirds vote by the fourth. Raymond Moley, a Columbia University professor of public law, and Samuel I. Rosenman, who had served as Roosevelt's counsel at Albany, prepared an acceptance speech. As the governor made a dramatic airplane flight from Albany to Chicago to accept the nomination, Rosenman did some last-minute polishing on the speech, adding the conclusion "I pledge you, I pledge myself, to a new deal for the American people." These words were the ones to be best remembered, and New Deal came to identify the whole Roosevelt administration, particularly the domestic part of it dealing with recovery and reform.

The Democratic platform of 1932 was actually conservative. It advocated a balanced budget, a lower tariff, the repeal of prohibition, extension of federal credit to states to fight unemployment, agricultural relief, and old-age and unemployment insurance. The candidate, crippled from polio but filled with enthusiasm and energy, was able to dramatize these recommendations and to make them sound much more novel than they were. Garner, the candidate for Vice-President, urged Roosevelt not to make an extended speaking tour. "All you have got to do is stay alive until election day," Garner said. It was probably true. About all the Republicans did was to reaffirm their contention that their methods of fighting the depression would work if given enough time. Hoover dolefully predicted that the Democrats would ruin the economy with federal controls and individual initiative would disappear. Disregarding Garner's advice, Roosevelt traveled widely, spoke often, and charmed millions with a jaunty pooh-poohing of Hoover's pessimism. The election was a walkaway. Hoover carried only six states, with an electoral vote of 59 against his opponent's 472. The Democrats also won both houses of Congress by large majorities. Clearly

This New Yorker *cover was to appear on the day Hoover escorted F.D.R. to his inauguration. It was withdrawn because of the attempted assassination two weeks earlier.*

the American people were ready to throw away the old hand of economic cards and to accept a new deal.

"The Hundred Days"

During the four months between the election and the inauguration (the Twentieth Amendment, ratified in this interim, considerably shortened it for future elections), conditions became even more desperate. Factories continued to lay off workers; some closed down completely as production dropped to the lowest level since 1914. The arteries of commerce grew more constricted, and hundreds of offices carried out no more than routine duties. Some 15,000,000 were unemployed. Farmers, militant and angry, forcibly prevented foreclosures on their land. Many of those who had any money were hoarding it. Already, on October 31, the governor of Nevada had declared a 12-day bank "holiday" to allow banks in his state to adjust to the worsening situation. This was followed during the winter by forced closings in Louisiana, Michigan, Maryland, and New York. By Inauguration Day, most of the banks were closed on a holiday basis or operating only part time.

On that rainy March 4, Roosevelt made his inaugural address to a thoroughly frightened nation. Characteristically, he struck an optimistic note, declaring that the country was fundamentally sound, that the situation could be and would be improved. "The only thing we have to fear is fear itself," he said, "—nameless, unreasoning, unjustified terror which paralyzes needed efforts to convert retreat into advance." He outlined a program of putting men back to work even if the government itself had to recruit them, of waging war upon the depression as if the nation had been invaded by a foreign foe, and of using broad executive powers to a degree hitherto unknown to Americans. The assertiveness of his proposals electrified a nation desolated by uncertainty. The people—Democrats and even most Republicans—were willing and eager to give him a chance. The day after his inauguration, a Sunday, Roosevelt went into action. He declared a four-day bank holiday, to start the next day. He called Congress into a special session.

Congress met on Thursday, March 9; it adjourned on June 16 after a history-making period that became known as the Hundred Days. It was hardly less exciting than the Hundred Days between Napoleon's return from Elba and the Battle of Waterloo, from which it took its name. During those eventful weeks, Roosevelt shepherded 15 major bills through Congress, made a number of important speeches, and ran the new administration like an accomplished ringmaster. By the time Congress had ended the special session, there was talk of the "Roosevelt Revolution," although the only revolutionary aspect of it had been its speed. Most of the new laws were designed to get the national machine off dead center and to start it up again; none were intended to overturn it.

The "fireside chat" is born

The first law to emerge from the Hundred Days was for financial first aid. On March 9, the Emergency Banking Relief Act was passed almost unanimously by Congress—the House debating it 38 minutes, the Senate three hours—and signed into law that night. It called in all gold

The sense of hopelessness, of endlessly waiting for a call that is not going to come, is caught in this painting by Isaac Soyer of an employment agency in 1937.

and provided for reopening banks as soon as federal inspectors could approve their condition. On March 12, in the first of his famous fireside chats —informal speeches by radio from the White House—Roosevelt lucidly explained the banking actions he was taking. "It is safer to keep your money in a reopened bank than under the mattress," he said. Within a few days, banks began to go back into business. By March 16, three-quarters of the Federal Reserve banks were reopened. Even the the stock market came to life.

Encouraged by the alacrity with which Congress had responded, Roo-sevelt pressed on, requesting more legislation. He asked for and got a cut in federal salaries and a reduction of payments and allowances to veterans. Then came legislative approval of a Civilian Conservation Corps to provide work for 250,000 unemployed young men in a program for preserving the national forest resources. Work camps were soon set up on a quasi-military basis. The young men—between 18 and 25— were paid $30 a month and a total of 2,000,000 ultimately participated. Among continuing attempts to put money into circulation was the creation of the Federal Emergency Relief

Flood refugees were still frequent victims of rivers out of control when Jon Corbino painted the above scene in 1938. But in the Tennessee Valley, the Norris Dam (below) and others built by the TVA not only controlled the rivers but preserved and improved the land and provided a tremendous increase in the output of electrical power.

Administration and the granting of $500,000,000 to it for relief spending. Harry Hopkins, later to become one of Roosevelt's most trusted assistants, was head of the new agency.

Farm and home foreclosure had disrupted thousands of families. The President sought to help them by urging passage of the Emergency Farm Mortgage Act, which authorized Federal Land Banks to refinance farm mortgages, and by establishing the Home Owners Loan Corporation to save the family home from foreclosure. In three years the HOLC loaned about $3,000,000,000 to more than 1,000,000 home owners. In addition, the new administration broadened the powers of the Reconstruction Finance Corporation, established under Hoover, allowing it to buy stocks in banks as well as to loan them money.

Congress battles the depression

The Agricultural Adjustment Act of May 12, 1933, was the New Deal's major answer to the deep-rooted and now intensified problems of the agricultural economy. In the simplest terms, the act was designed to reduce agricultural surpluses by reducing the amount of acreage planted. The Secretary of Agriculture, Henry Wallace, was empowered to make agreements with individual farmers, giving them benefit payments to compensate for reduced planting. The money to pay for this land "rental" was to be realized from a tax collected from the processor of the product—the miller,

The National Recovery Administration emblem was displayed by all industries that were trying—by voluntary regulation of production and prices—to improve the economy.

for example, in the case of wheat. By this means, the government hoped to approach an ideal, or "parity," price for agricultural products. Generally, the parity price was that paid to farmers before World War I.

One of the more controversial pieces of legislation to come out of the Hundred Days was the act establishing the Tennessee Valley Authority on May 18. It was set up as an independent corporation with powers to build dams and power plants in the Tennessee Valley—an area covering Tennessee, Kentucky, North Carolina, Virginia, Mississippi, Georgia, and Alabama. The aim of the authority was the social and economic betterment of the region, a poor one by most American standards. Flood control, reforestation, land renewal, industrial diversification were among the goals envisioned in the TVA's establishment. Critics of the authority called it "socialistic" because of its unprecedented incursion into what had been primarily private sectors of the economy—the most intensive in American history if measured in terms of impact on a large geographical area. Supporters of the idea, which was eventually to gain the approval of many of its early critics, considered the TVA an exciting experiment that might pave the way for similar projects in other underdeveloped areas.

Within a few days of the TVA's passage, Congress created the Federal Securities Act, a forerunner of one establishing the Securities and Exchange Commission, which was aimed primarily at regulating the stock and bond markets to prevent price manipulations. On June 5, Congress took steps to move the United States away from a gold standard toward a controlled currency by voting the Gold Repeal Joint Resolution, canceling clauses in federal and private contracts that required payment in gold. Eleven days later, the government launched an all-out attack on a broad front of the economy. The National Industrial Recovery Act, passed June 16, 1933, combined two major thrusts —one, a public works program to provide an immediate stimulus; the other, formation of the National Recovery Administration. This agency, known as the NRA, was designed to organize all possible industries into one giant effort somewhat similar to that of World War I. The industries themselves, through their representatives, drew up codes of competition and agreed to certain practices recommended by the administration. The attractiveness of the plan to industry lay in the fact that all antitrust activities were to be suspended and they were free to engage in a gigantic price-fixing program. On the other hand, industries were required to abide by new rules for maximum hours and minimum pay and to eliminate child labor. The labor provisions of the NRA were regarded as giving a strong impetus to the labor movement.

Membership in the NRA was voluntary, although great pressure was put upon those who did not want to join. Those who did could display a placard bearing a Blue Eagle. Above the eagle was the inscription "NRA" and, below, the sentence "We Do Our Part." General Hugh S. Johnson, a colorful former army officer, became NRA administrator. Within four months of the Blue Eagle's birth, "Old Ironpants"—as Johnson was called because of his stubborness and determination—claimed that 96% of industry and commerce were under its wings.

Thus did the New Deal begin. Its first days were hectic, tumultuous, and sometimes confusing even to those in charge. But the new administration was propelled by the feeling that something had to be done—and there was, however anyone looked at it, no question about there being action.

F.D.R.

He was one of the best-loved and best-hated Presidents in American history. To some, he was "that man in the White House" and a "traitor to his class." To others, he was the symbol of all their hopes for a better chance for their children, a bigger share in the nation's wealth, a richer life. For these, Roosevelt was a popular first name for their sons in the '30s. He led his country during its harshest depression and during its grimmest war. To what degree his New Deal measures should be credited with pulling the United States out of the depression is still a matter of debate among economists, but there can be no doubt that the New Deal did permanently alter the social structure of the country. It helped make labor more powerful economically and politically. It taught the farmer to look to Washington for help of the kind that industry had been getting in tariffs and subsidies for years. The aristocrat whose family coat of arms (above) carries the motto "He who sows shall reap" planted many of the seeds of change in the society into which he was born.

THE
BACKGROUND
OF A
PRESIDENT

Franklin Delano was born in 1882 to James Roosevelt and his wife Sara Delano. Father was 41, a railroad magnate, almost twice the age of his second wife, daughter of an old New England family grown rich in the China trade. What sort of childhood produced a man who could triumph over the greatest personal and national adversities? He was an only child. His father seems to have been quite the opposite of the heavy 19th-century parent, and instead a man capable of a close relationship with his son. His mother adored him and, from the time he was born, saved childhood mementos with an enthusiasm that suggests she either sensed he would be great or intended he should be. The boy's home (above) was a sprawling house on a bluff over the Hudson River at Hyde Park, New York, and although it was large and well attended, it must have seemed modest indeed compared to the Vanderbilt mansion only a few miles to the north. Young Franklin's advantages, then, were not those of a child who feels he will never have to make his own way.

HIS FOREBEARS AND HIS BOYHOOD

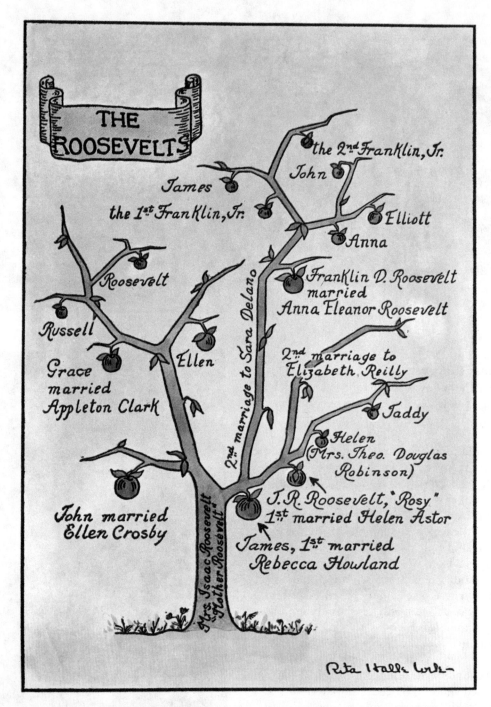

Both sides of the family had long been in America. Phillipe De La Noye (later Delano) came to New England in 1621, Claes van Rosenvelt to New Amsterdam in the 1640s. This family tree begins with F.D.R.'s grandmother.

Franklin is a little over two (above). He was raised by nurses and a mother who constantly fretted about his health.

When Franklin's father took him to see Grover Cleveland in 1887 (below), the President said, "I hope, young man, when you grow up, you'll never be President."

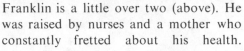

Until he was 14, he was educated at home by tutors. Besides doing well in studies, he became a devoted bird watcher and stamp collector and a good horseman. Finally, his somewhat possessive mother consented to his going away to a preparatory school—Groton. He went from there to Harvard, and at both schools was considered a good, if not brilliant, student. In 1905, just after entering Columbia Law School, he was married to his fifth cousin, Anna Eleanor Roosevelt, Theodore's niece.

1191

F.D.R.

THE
RISING
YOUNG
MAN

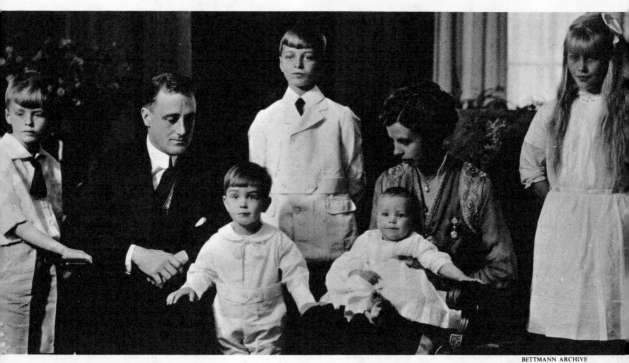

HARRIS & EWING

Until 1910, he and his young bride (above left, in profile) lived the life of a comfortable New York couple with an inherited income. Then the Democrats offered Roosevelt the nomination for state senator. He won, and in 1912 went to the Democratic national convention to fight for the nomination of Woodrow Wilson for President. Wilson won, and subsequently was elected. He appointed F.D.R. his Assistant Secretary of the Navy (right), and the growing family (left) moved to Washington in 1913. With a love of the sea that went back to childhood—and no doubt recalling that his cousin Teddy had held the same post before going to the Presidency—Roosevelt served until the end of World War I with a distinction that led Wilson to refuse him a commission when he asked to go on more active service. He was well enough known so that, in 1920, a worn-out Democratic convention, which had gone through 44 ballots to nominate James M. Cox of Ohio for President, made him their candidate for Vice-President. But the country wanted to get back to "normalcy" after the war years, and Cox and Roosevelt lost to Harding and Coolidge. Nevertheless, the future appeared bright for the young man of 38. A near-tragic setback was, however, less than one year away.

TRAGEDY AND TRIUMPH

In August, 1921, Roosevelt, back in law practice, was vacationing on Campobello Island, off the coast of Maine, where his father had built a summer house. He went to bed one night with a chill and awoke the next morning with a high fever and with his legs paralyzed from the hips down. It was polio. Until 1924 he was out of politics while he fought to learn to use crutches (left) and swam in the healing waters of Warm Springs, Georgia (below). By May, 1924, he was able to hobble to the platform of Madison Square Garden and nominate Al Smith for President. Smith lost the nomination, but Roosevelt was back on the political scene. By 1928, when he was able to walk with a cane (right), he won the governorship of New York. In 1932, he was the Democratic nominee for President, and a depression-ridden country, despairing of the Republicans' lack of action, sent him to the White House with a landslide victory.

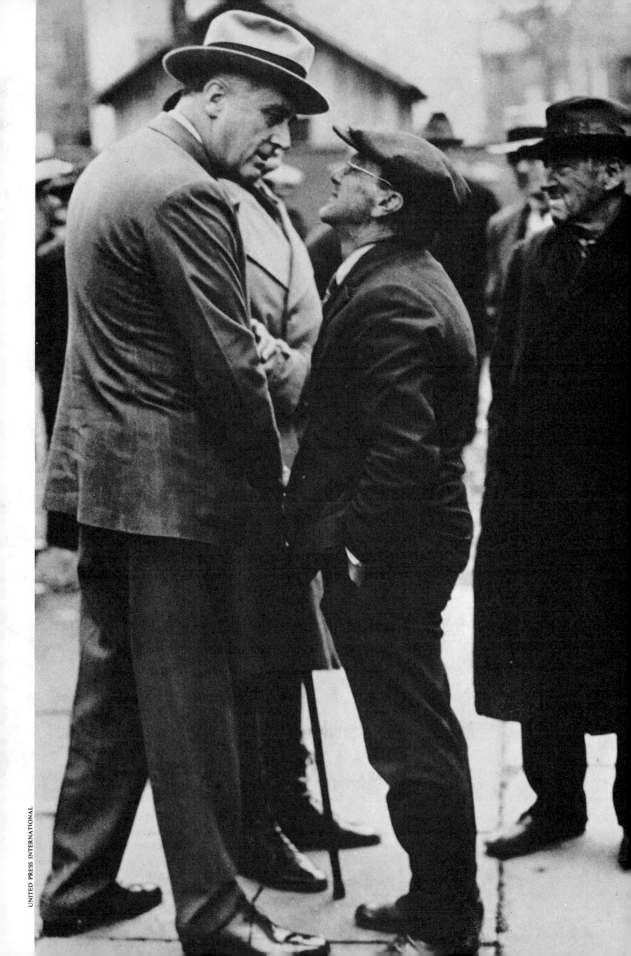

THE INAUGURATION OF FRANKLII

AN HEROIC PANORAMA DEPICTING THE HIGH CEREMONY ON THE CAPITOL PLA

Done into Full Color in the Memorial Manner by Miguel Covarrubias, Painter Extraordinary a

1 President Franklin D. Roosevelt
2 Chief Justice Charles Evans Hughes
3 Mrs. Franklin D. Roosevelt
4 Vice-President John N. Garner
5 Ex-President Herbert Hoover
6 Mrs. Herbert Hoover
7 Ex-Vice-President Charles Curtis
8 Alfred E. Smith
9 James A. Farley
10 Raymond Moley
11 Louis Howe
12 Senator Joseph T. Robinson
13 Bernard M. Baruch
14 Owen D. Young
15 Senator William G. McAdoo
16 Governor Albert C. Ritchie
17 Senator Claude A. Swanson
18 Senator Pat Harrison
19 Governor Herbert H. Lehman
20 Senator Thomas J. Walsh
21 John W. Davis
22 Senator Carter Glass
23 Norman H. Davis
24 Newton D. Baker
25 Henry L. Stimson
26 Andrew W. Mellon
27 Ogden L. Mills
28 J. P. Morgan
29 Ambassador Paul Claudel
30 Ambassador Sir Ronald Lindsay
31 and 32 Oriental Ambassadors
33 Mark Sullivan
34 Walter Lippmann
35 Gentlemen of the Press
36 General John J. Pershing
37 The Forgotten Man
38 The United States Navy

. ROOSEVELT

WASHINGTON ON MARCH 4, 1933

toriographer to the Court on the Potomac

THE FIRST FAMILY

THE PRESIDENT'S MOTHER—Although she stayed mostly at Hyde Park, Sara Roosevelt's notions of *noblesse oblige* had a strong influence on the policies her son followed. At her death in 1941, he said that perhaps it was all for the best—she would not have liked the postwar world.

THE PRESIDENT'S WIFE—Eleanor Roosevelt was both legs and eyes for her husband. Her wide-ranging trips around the country became a standard target for humorists, but she was a skilled observer and F.D.R. relied heavily on her frank reports even when the two of them differed.

THE PRESIDENT—In addition to being a master at the give-and-take of the traditional Presidential press conference, Roosevelt developed a new technique for bringing his views to the public—the "fireside chat." He made the first of these informal talks over the radio only eight days after taking office and used them regularly to explain programs and bolster confidence.

A NATURAL FOR CARICATURISTS

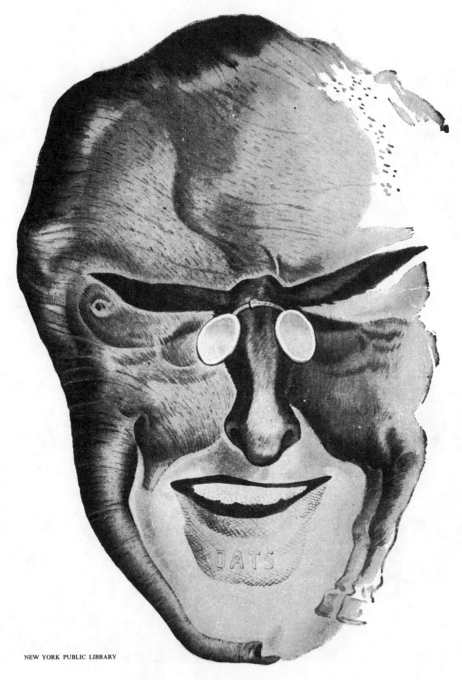

F.D.R. was a caricaturist's delight. At the left, *Vanity Fair,* the famous satiric magazine, showed him as a happy cowboy riding high on a horse shaped like the United States. Above, the newspaper *PM* sees him as both Democrat and Republican, combining donkey (right) and elephant (left).

LIFE AND DEATH OF AN EAGLE

Above, *Vanity Fair* has the President as a chef serving up the Blue Eagle, symbol of the National Recovery Administration (NRA). At the right, he is still the ringmaster in control of the animals of the political zoo, but the Blue Eagle, struck down by a Supreme Court decision as unconstitutional, limps along on a crutch at the bottom of the painting.

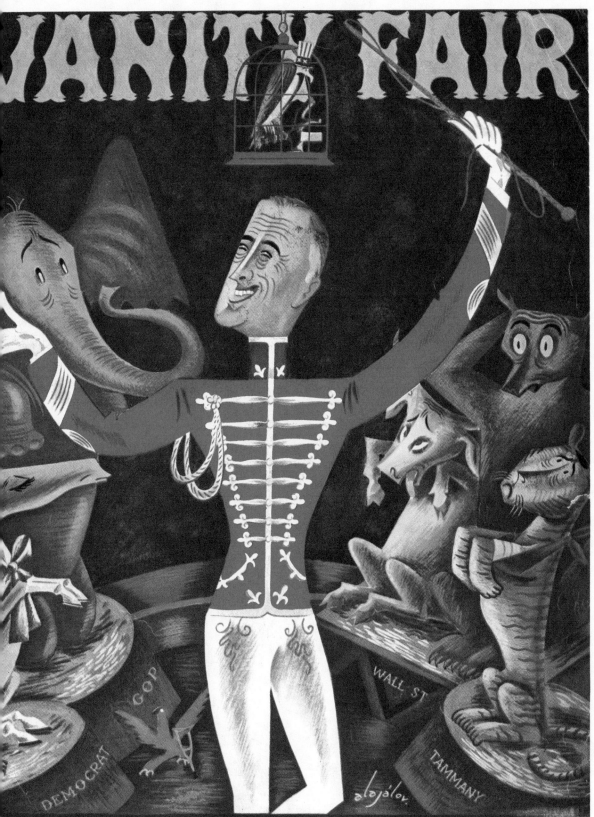

VANITY FAIR

BOUQUETS AND BRICKBATS

The "victory version" of a famous face—Uncle Sam's
SHAW IN THE WASHINGTON STAR

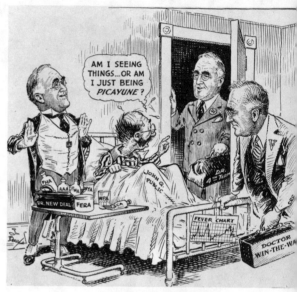

BERRYMAN IN THE WASHINGTON STAR

But we've got something to show for it!
TALBURT IN THE NEW YORK WORLD-TELEGRAM

Uncle: "But, doctor, isn't it time she went on a diet?"
MARCUS IN THE NEW YORK TIMES

"Mother, Wilfred wrote a bad word!"
MCKAY IN ESQUIRE

"Better let that guy go"
HERBLOCK © CARTOON

No, dearie, he isn't running!
TALBURT IN THE WASHINGTON NEWS

How's that again?
TALBURT IN THE WASHINGTON NEWS

F.D.R. gave the cartoonists plenty to work with. The jaunty cigarette holder (facing page) was a favorite trademark. To the right of it, his many roles during his long tenure are commented upon. And the two drawings at the bottom take opposite sides on the question of government spending. On this page, there is a criticism of political influence in the Works Progress Administration (WPA) and, at the bottom, jibes about the third and fourth terms.

THE COMMANDER IN CHIEF DIES

He died on April 12, 1945, at his retreat at Warm Springs, Georgia. He was having his portrait painted when he suddenly fell back unconscious. The famous, confident smile (right) was gone forever, and if a few Roosevelt-haters drank toasts, the cartoon at the left expressed the feelings of most men and women around the world.

UNITED PRESS INTERNATIONAL

Today's Army-Navy Casualty List

Washington, Apr. 13.—Following are the latest casualties in the military services, including next-of-kin.

ARMY-NAVY DEAD

ROOSEVELT, Franklin. D., Commander-in-Chief, wife, Mrs. Anna Eleanor Roosevelt, the White House.

Navy Dead

DECKER, Carlos Anthony, Fireman 1c. Sister, Mrs. Elizabeth Decker Metz, 16 Concord Pl., Concord, S. I.

SEILER, Edwin Norton, Lt. Mother, Mrs. Evelyn Norton Seiler, Fifth Av. Bank.

STAINTON, Alfred, Harold, Ensign.

NEW YORK PUBLIC LIBRARY

CULVER PICTURES

Franklin Roosevelt

★

DIED IN ACTION 4-12-45

CHAPTER 41

YEAR BY YEAR, 1929–1939

The decade between 1929 and 1939 was a somewhat gray period of American history, because so many aspects of existence were tinged by the economic troubles that gripped the country. Yet other, more cheerful hues were discernible; life inevitably went on, and progress in many areas was made in spite of economic reversal. Perhaps as good a way as any for studying the era is to look at it chronologically, noting the events that moved by against the ever-present backdrop of the great depression.

In the fall of 1929, the nation became aware of certain wonders that were appearing on the scene. In New York, demolition crews were hammering down the old Waldorf-Astoria to make space for the world's tallest skyscraper, the Empire State Building. In a less concrete but no less ambitious field, "talkies"—motion pictures with fairly well-coordinated sound tracks —began to look like something more than imperfect novelties. Al Jolson, the vaudeville singer whose booming tones

In Vanity Fair, Herbert Hoover emerges from retirement with his new book expressing disaffection for the New Deal.

echoed in movie theaters throughout the land, had pioneered the talking picture with *The Jazz Singer,* and was now appearing in *Say It With Songs.* The first Walt Disney cartoon had recently appeared, followed by Mickey Mouse, soon to be world-famous.

And there was radio. Still in its infancy as an information and entertainment medium (almost anything but a crystal set cost over $100), it nevertheless brought sound, mostly music, to 12,000,000 families who already owned receivers. Parents were beginning to worry about their children spending too much time glued to the sputtering speakers, while a new comic twosome called Amos 'n' Andy was holding the interests of the parents themselves. Another mechanism, the automobile, was passing 25,000,-000 in registrations—one car for every five people in the United States—and there were over 500,000 miles of surfaced roads for it to roll on.

Above all, figuratively and literally, there was the airplane, wonder of wonders. In 1927, Charles A. Lindbergh had flown the Atlantic alone in a single-engine plane to become a national hero. Congress had passed an

In June, 1930, Richard E. Byrd, sitting beside New York's official host, Grover Whalen, is given a ticker-tape parade in honor of his flight over the South Pole.

act that provided for the construction of an aircraft carrier. In 1929, one month after Black Tuesday, the stock market's worst day, Richard E. Byrd flew over the South Pole from a base in Little America.

Prohibition, the "noble experiment" that had spawned bootleggers, speakeasies, bathtub gin, and other lurid features of the postwar era, was entering its final stage of collapse. The laws designed to prevent the sale of alcoholic beverages were being flagrantly ignored. Anyone who wanted a drink could get one at a speakeasy, as an unlawful drinking place was called. Liquor could be bought by the bottle from bootleggers, whose telephone numbers were often available on printed price lists. The news was soon to break that orders were being filled in the Senate office building—infor-

mation that probably confirmed more suspicions than it aroused.

The trailer, a house on wheels that could be towed by an automobile, was on display in New York. . . . Social realism was beginning to dominate the American art scene. . . . Flagpole-sitting was becoming passe. . . . Miniature golf was beginning to catch on. And so America approached the '30s, stunned by the stock market debacle but distracted from time to time from the ominous economic malady that seemed to be spreading.

1930

On March 13, it was announced that a ninth planet was revolving around the sun with the earth. Discovered at the Lowell Observatory at Flagstaff, Arizona, it was estimated to be about 10,000 miles in diameter and to take

250 earth-years to orbit the sun. It was named after the Greek god of Hades, Pluto. There would always, the discovery seemed to mean, be something new under the sun, and even with unemployment over 4,000,000, men continued to be sanguine about solving their worldly difficulties. One of the recurring searches of the '30s, bringing surges of hope and disillusionment, was for a workable means of world disarmament. On December 9, 1929, a method of adherence to the World Court by the United States—which had steadfastly stayed aloof from the court and its parent body, the League of Nations—had been agreed to and signed by an American charge d'affaires in Switzerland, but in 1935 the Senate rejected it.

On January 21, 1930, Secretary of State Henry L. Stimson sat down at a conference in London that was to take four months in seeking limitation on naval armaments and result in a partial agreement between the United States, Great Britain, and Japan. Five months later, the League of Nations—which, if it could not be accepted by the United States, was free to accept Americans—elected Frank B. Kellogg to the World Court. He had been co-author of the widely heralded Kellogg-Briand Pact, a treaty signed eventually by 62 nations, which provided for the "outlawry of war." Unfortunately, like many other agreements that relied on moral interpretations or world opinion for enforcement, this one proved to be almost completely ineffective. Nevertheless, it was widely hailed at the time as providing a basis for perpetual peace. Such being the enthusiasms of Americans, there was probably more immediate joy in 1930 over Robert Tyre "Bobby" Jones' capture of the four big titles in golf—the British and American Amateur and Open Championships. Another sports triumph for the United States came with the defeat of the British *Shamrock* by the *Enterprise* in the America Cup race that fall in Newport, Rhode Island.

1931

As if to confirm that America was no longer the land of frontiers, of hope and opportunity, 1931 was the first year in the nation's history in

The '30s were the great days of Mickey Mouse and other Walt Disney characters.

With a yearly income of millions from crime and vice, Al Capone seemed beyond the law until jailed for tax evasion in 1931.

A Harvard Law School graduate and practicing lawyer, Bobby Jones was the sports hero of 1930, winning the Big Four in golf.

which the number of people coming into it was smaller than the number leaving. The restrictive immigration laws were partly accountable, but the worldwide economic hardship was probably the major reason. Economic distress, however, did not stop what a leading British scientist called "one of the most important discoveries of the century." Announced in 1931, it was the discovery of deuterium, an isotope of hydrogen, by Dr. Harold C. Urey of Columbia University. "Heavy hydrogen" or "heavy water," as the isotope was called, had an atomic weight of two instead of ordinary hydrogen's one. Urey won the Nobel Prize for his discovery, which opened up new fields of knowledge and experimentation leading to unforeseen gains in atomic research—and eventually to controlled

nuclear fission, with all its implications and applications.

Otherwise, 1931 was marked by few innovations. Yale University, to be sure, dropped Latin as a requirement for its bachelor of arts degree, reflecting in part the pragmatism that was continuing to gain ground in American education. And Congress took time out from considering the woes of the land to designate *The Star-Spangled Banner* as the national anthem. The excitement of the air age was still present, and Americans were elated when Wiley Post and Harold Gatty took off in their monoplane, the *Winnie Mae,* for a trip around the world, and returned from the opposite direction eight days, 15 hours, and 51 minutes later. That fall, Al Capone, recently released from a Phila-

While working at Columbia University, Dr. Harold C. Urey was awarded the Nobel Prize in 1934 for isolating heavy hydrogen.

Wiley Post and Harold Gatty stand in front of the plane in which they made their 1931 round-the-world trip in less than nine days.

delphia jail where he had been serving a year's sentence for carrying a pistol, was clapped in a federal prison for income-tax evasion. Capone had long had worldwide notoriety as Chicago's leading gang chief. The sentence this time was 11 years, with a fine of $50,000. John Dillinger, a bank robber and holdup specialist, was Public Enemy No. 1 until he was shot down walking out of a movie theater in Chicago in 1934, when he tried to battle it out with a group of Department of Justice agents. The G-men, as the agents were called, went on to track down "Pretty Boy" Floyd and "Baby Face" Nelson.

In the meantime, a more ominous lawbreaker misbehaved blatantly and no one did anything but protest. On September 18, 1931, in clear violation

of the Kellogg-Briand Pact and the covenant of the League of Nations, Japan invaded Manchuria. There was considerable American sentiment in favor of an economic boycott, but President Hoover opposed it. On December 10, the League of Nations appointed a commission, including one American representative, to investigate the invasion; the commission's report condemned Japan, which gave notice of withdrawal from the league. So darkened the western horizon of America's foreign relations. The eastern horizon would show its danger clouds soon.

1932

The major national news event of 1932 was the kidnapping of Colonel Charles A. Lindbergh's 19-month-

Amelia Earhart was the first woman to fly alone across the Atlantic, in 1932, and from Hawaii to California, in 1935.

Hattie Caraway, whose husband was a Senator from Arkansas, became the first woman ever elected to the United States Senate.

old son. On the night of March 1, the child was taken from an upstairs bedroom while Lindbergh and his wife sat downstairs in their Hopewell, New Jersey, home. The public reaction was one of shock and outrage. A week after the crime, with no clues to the kidnapper despite one of the most intensive man hunts in the country's history, a Dr. John F. Condon received a letter in answer to an advertisement he had put in the *Bronx Home News*. The advertisement, taken on his own initiative, stated his willingness to serve as an intermediary for ransoming the child. The letter to Condon contained markings identical to those on a ransom note left in the Lindbergh child's room. On March 12, Condon arranged to meet with the letter writer, and after further identification had proved that he was definitely involved in the kidnapping, $50,-000 was left for him in a Bronx cemetery. On May 12, the boy's body was found half-buried in a wooded area about five miles from the Lindbergh home. It was more than two years before the kidnapper was identified and arrested, and the trial that followed, in 1935, was as great a news event as the kidnapping itself had been. The evidence presented was circumstantial and dramatic, and the defendant—Bruno Richard Hauptmann, an illegal immigrant from Germany—pleaded innocence until his death, by electrocution. The crime brought a stiffening of state kidnapping laws and legislation extending federal jurisdiction in kidnapping cases.

During 1932, science took a giant step toward harnessing the atom. The first practical cyclotron was built by the University of California's Ernest O. Lawrence, who received the Nobel Prize for his work in 1939. In politics, a tradition was broken when the first woman Senator, Hattie Caraway, was elected in Arkansas. The first big exhibition of skiing in the United States was seen at Lake Placid, New York, where the Olympic Winter Games were held, and that year Amelia Earhart became the first woman to complete a solo flight across the Atlantic.

The World Disarmament Conference, sponsored by the League of Nations, met in 1932 at Geneva—with 61 nations, including the United States, participating. President Hoover, recognizing the disastrous alternatives to disarmament, sent several radical pro-

The small town of Flemington, New Jersey, became the center of the nation's interest in 1935 when the trial of the kidnapper of the Lindbergh baby was held.

posals with his representatives. He first asked that all offensive weapons be abolished, and when this idea was rejected, he urged that all armaments be reduced by one-third. France, with an eye on mounting militarist sentiment in Germany, fed by Adolf Hitler's National Socialist Party, was cool to the proposal, and little came out of the conference. As Japan had attacked Shanghai four days before the conference got under way, the arguments had an air of tragic tardiness in any case.

At home, a more significant stride in the application of law to man's contentiousness was made in the so-called First Scottsboro Case (*Powell vs. Alabama*). The Supreme Court ordered the retrial of eight Negroes convicted of rape, declaring they had not been properly represented by counsel, as required by the due-process provision of the Fourteenth Amendment. The case was one of a number reaching back to 1925 that extended the provisions of the Fourteenth Amendment to cover personal as well as property rights, and marked, according to some legal historians, a broad philosophical shift in this major area of Supreme Court concern.

1933

F.D.R. had narrowly escaped death two weeks before his inauguration when, on February 15, an assassin fired several shots at him in Miami and hit and killed Mayor Anton Cermak of Chicago instead. This ex-

Through negotiations with Maxim Litvinov, the United States recognized the Soviet Union in 1933 for the first time since 1917.

pression of anti-Roosevelt feeling had no apparent restraining effect on the new President as his New Deal boomed into being. Around its major economic and sociological developments, and inevitably influenced by them, were a number of others, overshadowed by the main drama of the time but of historic importance. The gradual withdrawal of United States military forces from the Latin American political scene was stepped up in 1933, when the last marines left Nicaragua. On August 7, the United States signed an agreement with Haiti for the withdrawal, in 1934, of the marines from that country. In October, Panama's commercial rights in the Canal Zone were outlined in an agreement between the United States and Panama. Finally, the Montevideo Conference denied the right of any state to intervene in the "internal or external affairs of another"—a new attitude in inter-American relations from that time, and one by which the United States, in effect, limited its influence in the fluid politics of its weaker hemispheric neighbors. All these actions tended to give substance to Roosevelt's inaugural declaration that "In the field of world policy I would dedicate this nation to the policy of the good neighbor." After the Montevideo Conference had implemented this good-neighbor policy in hemispheric relations, Roosevelt declared, on December 28, "The definite policy of the United States from now on is one opposed to armed intervention." Never before, and seldom since, has the United States been so popular among Latin Americans.

Another major event in America's foreign relations took place when, at Roosevelt's request, the Soviet Union's Commissar for Foreign Affairs, Maxim Litvinov, arrived in Washington on November 7. In a formal exchange of notes, the United States recognized the Soviet Union after having refused to do so for 16 years since the Bolshevik Revolution. As part of the recognition agreements, the U.S.S.R. promised to discontinue anti-American propaganda and attempts to interfere in United States domestic affairs—a pledge that was scrupulously ignored in times to come.

The first legal break in prohibition came in early 1933 when the Beer and Wine Revenue Act went into effect, legalizing beer and wine with a maximum alcoholic content of 3.2% by weight. The main effect of the law was to provide tax revenue; most lovers of weak beer and wine were already being amply supplied without legal

Virtually a dictator in Louisiana, Huey Long proposed a Share Our Wealth program to tax the wealthy and give to the poor.

blessing. On December 5, the Twenty-first Amendment to the Constitution went into effect with ratification by a 36th state, Utah. By repealing the prohibition amendment, the United States took itself legally "off the wagon," after 14 years of trying enforced abstinence and failing at it.

Meanwhile, on October 17, Albert Einstein arrived in the United States, fleeing growing anti-Semitic oppression in his native Germany—which, under her new chancellor, Adolf Hitler, had declared her intention of resigning from the League of Nations. On November 7, the city of New York elected a reform mayor, Fiorello La Guardia, the "Little Flower," whose ability, force of personality, and eccentricity of character made him one

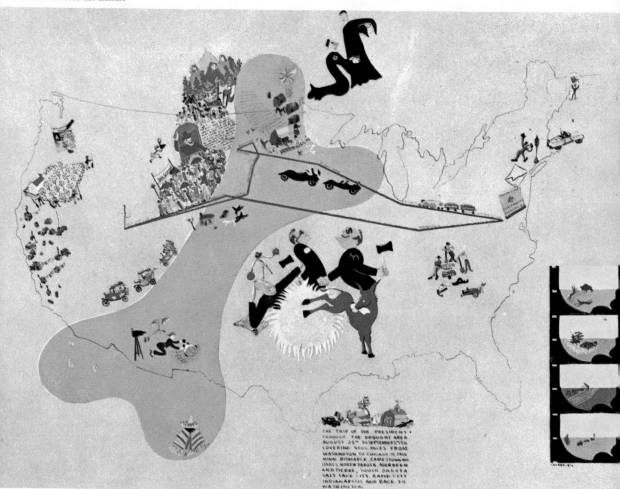

President Roosevelt's trip in 1936 to the drought area, characterized as dry as a bone, is outlined on this cartoon map drawn by a member of his staff.

Dust was the dread enemy of this farmer in Cimarron County, Oklahoma, in 1936.
Storms would last for days, burying houses and barns and killing animals and crops.

of the best-liked figures on the political scene, and often provided comic relief to the solemn drama of the '30s. On the same day, nature made its own gloomy contribution to this troubled year. The first of the great dust storms swept over North Dakota, sending its dismal, choking clouds as far east as Albany, New York.

1934

In May, 1934, another giant dust storm blew through Texas, Oklahoma, Kansas, and Colorado and carried away 300,000,000 tons of precious topsoil from those states, leaving thousands of families destitute, with no fertile earth left to farm. Beset further by foreclosures on their heavily mortgaged homes and by landowners' attempts to make farming more efficient by consolidating small plots

into huge tracts, many found themselves dispossessed of home and land. Thousands who had automobiles crowded family and possessions aboard and drove west. (These pathetic migrants were later the subject of *The Grapes of Wrath,* a moving novel by John Steinbeck, a 1962 Nobel Prize winner.) Their destination was usually California, where many residents resentfully felt they had enough troubles of their own without the influx of "Okies" and "Arkies."

Several Californians were among those who offered bold solutions to these troubles, which were nationwide in scope. The solutions were centered as much on personalities as ideas; they were not always explicit, and they usually appealed to people more desperate than discriminating. There was Dr. Francis E. Townsend of Long

An Arkansas cotton farmer and his wife, desperately poor, stand helplessly before their fields almost barren with the drought, in a drawing by Bernarda Bryson.

Beach, California, whose Old-Age Revolving Pension promised $200 a month to every unemployed person over 60. Upton Sinclair, running as Democratic candidate for governor of California in 1934, championed EPIC—End Poverty In California. This was a program of epic proportions that envisaged organizing the unemployed into groups producing for one another. Sinclair barely lost the election. Huey Long, near-dictator of Louisiana, proposed to fellow Senators his Share Our Wealth program, which by taxing the rich would enable every family to have "a homestead allowance, free of debt, of not less than one-third the average family wealth of the country."

On another front, the growing disenchantment with the recent past was heightened by the Senate's Nye Committee investigations. Chairman Gerald P. Nye led the committee through a malodorous maze of bankers, munitions makers, and government officials, leaving the country with the uneasy impression that if the profit motive was not the main one in World War I, it was never far from the front. This impression, and the growing isolationist sentiment that it fostered, was further expressed and strengthened by a widely read book

To flee drought areas in Oklahoma and Arkansas, people migrated to California, as has this family arriving with all their belongings in San Fernando in 1935.

published in 1935—Walter Millis' *Road to War: America, 1914-1917*— which attempted to explain why it had been a great mistake for the United States to enter World War I. Such sentiment seemed ironic when related to something ominous that happened just before the end of 1934. On December 29, Japan renounced two treaties hopefully aimed at limiting naval armaments—an undisguised expression of its growing military designs in the Pacific.

1935

As if propelled by the notion that it could unilaterally disengage itself from world problems, the United States Senate voted again against adherence to the World Court. And on August 31, in an attempt to avoid the first link in the Nye Committee's suggested chain of steps leading to war, Congress passed the First Neutrality Act, forbidding transportation of munitions to warring countries. The act was applied a little more than a month later when Italy attacked Ethiopia. During the year, Technicolor came to the movie screen, and the WPA Federal Arts Project came to the aid of hungry artists, many of whom had a built-in predilection for the "Ash Can School" of painting—stark slum scenes being a favorite subject. Plays expressed the same preoccupation with social messages in this period. Clifford Odets was among the more successful socially conscious playwrights with *Paradise Lost, Awake and Sing,* and *Waiting for Lefty*, all in 1935. Lillian Hellman's *The Children's Hour* (1934) and Robert E. Sherwood's *The Petrified Forest* (1935) had already reached Broadway. The WPA Federal Theater Project was soon to bring legitimate theater to the smaller towns and cities of America, and in the later '30s it would tackle the social problem head-on, dramatizing headlines in such plays as *Triple A Ploughed Under* (1936), *Power* (1937), and *One Third*

of a Nation (1938). In the world of fiction, William Faulkner was gaining worldwide praise for his naturalistic novels portraying for the most part sordid slices of low-class life in the South. Within this realm, Erskine Caldwell had recently contributed *Tobacco Road*. The third book of James Farrell's *Studs Lonigan* trilogy appeared in 1935, looking at squalor farther north, in Chicago. Even in religion a special social consciousness was gaining ground in 1935, as American Protestants followed the lead of Reinhold Niebuhr, the theologian, in synthesizing social liberalism with a type of Biblical fundamentalism. "I got plenty of nothin' and nothin's plenty for me,"

After crossing the Atlantic in 1937, the Hindenburg, *a German dirigible with 97 passengers aboard, mysteriously exploded as it landed at Lakehurst, New Jersey.*

A formidable labor leader for the miners for over 15 years, John L. Lewis founded the C.I.O. in 1935, was its first president.

Startling the entire world in 1936, King Edward VIII of England abdicated his crown and in June, 1937, married Wallis Simpson.

sang another sort of contemporary philosopher in a sad and stirring new opera of 1935. It was a brilliantly successful incorporation of jazz idioms into a "serious" work—George Gershwin's *Porgy and Bess.*

1936

If many of the artists of the period —especially those subsidized by the government—used bold, unsentimental strokes, it was by no means certain that the people preferred portraits of grim reality in the midst of such reality itself. By far the most successful book of the decade appeared in 1936; within six months it sold over 1,000,000 copies. This was Margaret Mitchell's *Gone With the Wind,* a thick, romantic novel of Southern love and heroism in Civil War days. If the ap-

peal was escapist, it was understandable enough; there was still a good deal worth escaping from as the depression moved into its sixth year.

Social strife was beginning to manifest itself in bitter, prolonged strikes. Through them, the labor unions sought to strengthen their position, while management, feeling its prerogatives being encroached upon, resisted firmly. Encouraged by New Deal labor policies, union membership (apart from company unions often set up to sidestep labor laws) rose to between 4,000,000 and 5,000,000 by 1936. The American Federation of Labor, based on the old trade and craft unions, was the major national organization. In August, 1936, unions associated with the Committee for Industrial Organization of the A.F.L.

Based upon one of the best-selling novels in history, Gone With the Wind *filled the screen for three hours with the Civil War, Vivian Leigh, and Clark Gable. Released in 1939, it is still among the 25 top money-making films of all time.*

had been suspended from the parent body. They were actively seeking more members in 1936, and recruiting was being done along broad industrial lines rather than by specialties. The labor unrest, which was to be severe for many months to come, exploded in the fall of 1936 in a giant strike of maritime workers. All West Coast ports were idle as 39,000 workers walked off their jobs there. The strike spread to Eastern and Gulf ports, and it was nearly three months before it was settled. More significant as a pattern for future strikes was one that began December 30 and ended 44 days later, paralyzing 60 factories in 14 states. This was the United Automobile Workers strike for recognition by General Motors. Here was a classic sitdown strike in which U.A.W. mem-

bers just about took over the plants in which they worked. When police tried to prevent food from being brought into a General Motors plant at Flint, Michigan, a battle ensued in which buckshot and tear gas were used, and pipes, bottles, and other objects hurled. The National Guard was called out. The strikers were threatened with jail sentences and stiff fines, but they held their ground. Meanwhile, thousands of union members and sympathizers crowded into Flint armed with makeshift weapons. To avoid a battle General Motors gave in, recognizing U.A.W. in 17 of its plants.

1937

Partly inspired by the U.A.W.'s success, unions staged some 4,500 strikes in 1937, although one of the significant labor events of the year was a strike that was averted. On March 2, 1937, the newspapers announced, to the astonishment of many workers and businessmen, that the United States Steel Company—after discussions with the C.I.O.'s bushy-browed president John L. Lewis—had recognized a unit of the C.I.O as an agent of its workers. Smaller steel companies failed to follow the giant's lead that year, however. Labor agitation growing out of strikes against three companies resulted in 10 deaths in one South Chicago skirmish. The strikers lost this battle, and the labor movement in general was slowed down as the recession of 1937–38 undermined union bargaining positions.

In 1937, the Golden Gate Bridge was completed in San Francisco, and the giant German dirigible *Hindenburg* exploded at Lakehurst, New Jersey, on May 6, as it completed its first transatlantic flight of the year. Another casualty of the air age was Amelia Earhart, who was lost in a flight over the Pacific and never seen again. King Edward VIII, who had abdicated his throne and become the Duke of Windsor, married Wallis Warfield Simpson, an American divorcee. In Spain, the forces of Francisco Franco were attacking the last stronghold of Spanish loyalist resistance—Madrid. The Spanish dictator-to-be was aided by German and Italian "volunteers" and supplies, the loyalists by Russian counterparts plus a sampling of idealists from many countries. Remote though it seemed, the Spanish Civil War proved to be a devastating prelude to a larger conflict not far off.

1938

A year of American business recession, 1938 was one in which Europe appeared to be rushing headlong toward chaos. Both conditions were soon to be resolved by the most bru-

The symbols for the 1939 New York World's Fair on Long Island were the Perisphere and the Trylon, entered by a circular ramp.

tal and destructive war of all time. The roots of isolationist sentiment ran deep in the United States and seemed powerful enough to keep the nation clear of any European conflict that might grow out of Hitler's territorial ambitions. On the other hand, historical sympathy for France and England, together with a growing moral repugnance at Nazi actions and ideology and a concern for national defense, led America to take steps to prepare for the worst. In the Pacific, facing increasing Japanese threats to our island possessions, the United States Navy began war maneuvers in March, the second such maneuvers in a year. In May, Congress authorized a billion-dollar expansion of naval construction. An attempt by Roosevelt to gain British backing for a world conference to reduce armaments was rebuffed by Prime Minister Neville Chamberlain. But in September, the prime minister went to Munich and returned with what he thought meant "peace in our time"—an agreement to give Hitler what he wanted in Czechoslovakia in return for the Nazi leader's assurance that this was the end of Germany's territorial demands. (A Gallup poll showed that a majority of Americans approved Chamberlain's wishful settlement.) That fall, many Americans tuned in to a radio program that seemed to be a news broadcast of an invasion from Mars, and thousands of them panicked. Newspapers were flooded with telephone calls; in many towns,

people dashed into the streets and wandered around dazed and frightened. What they heard was merely a dramatization of H. G. Wells' *The War of the Worlds*, put on by Orson Welles, but the broadcast became famous as an example of the psychological effectiveness of mass communications—an effectiveness that across the ocean was being employed to stir a nation into offensive war.

1939

What the majority of Americans wanted and what they were likely to get appeared to be distressingly far apart in 1939. To be sure, a few straws in the wind promised an exciting future—the first public television broadcast, on April 30, from New York City's Empire State Building; the inauguration of the first regular transatlantic passenger air service, with 22 people flying from Long Island on June 28 and reaching Lisbon 23 hours and 52 minutes later; San Francisco's Golden Gate International Exposition and the New York World's Fair, with their confident visions of great things to come.

Although it was not for all to see, the handwriting was on the wall: The end of an era had come. The train of events that was leading Europe to war was drawing America inexorably closer—first to moral commitment, then to involvement, and finally, and inevitably, to participation on the side of Great Britain. The decade that began in anxiety ended the same way.

American Gothic. 1930. GRANT WOOD.

THE ARTIST'S AMERICA

The revitalized painting of the 20th century branched out in two directions. In one, artists modified the native tradition of realism in unprecedented ways. Rejecting the credo that only "beautiful" subjects were worthy of treatment, they reinterpreted the authentic American scene in its infinite variety with honest eyes and new excitement. Moved to a new social consciousness by the blight of the depression, Reginald Marsh, Philip Guston, and William Gropper protested evils and inequities. A more rural Americanism was the rallying point of the Midwestern regional painters like Grant Wood and John Steuart Curry. Following the lead of pioneer Edward Hopper, they defied New York as well as Paris and painted the Iowa and Kansas they knew and loved. In the other direction—European-influenced—lay abstraction and expressionism, which shows in the work of Joseph Stella, John Marin, Georgia O'Keeffe, and Stuart Davis. And in typical American fashion, many painters, Marsden Hartley and Charles Sheeler among them, excerpted elements of abstract art and adapted them to the native tradition of romantic realism. This portfolio is a sampling of what American artists did between the Roaring Twenties and World War II.

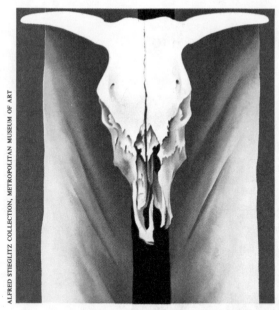

Cow's Skull, Red, White, and Blue. 1931
GEORGIA O'KEEFFE.

The variety of subject matter open to the American artist has been as diverse as the land. In a country where the form of the beautiful has not been dictated by the tastes of an elite, it has been left to the artist to define and determine what was beautiful. Georgia O'Keeffe was noted for her simplicity of style and her ability to imbue objects like the cow's skull at the left with a classic quality. Marsden Hartley painted many scenes of Maine, like the one below, with a rough, stern, blunt style that matched the landscape. Joseph Stella's conception of the Brooklyn Bridge at the right is one of the famous American paintings. In emphasizing the spirit of the bridge—its movement and strength—rather than representing it more literally, Stella has brought out its power to stir emotions.

Mt. Katahdin, Autumn No. 1. 1939–1940. MARSDEN HARTLEY.

The Brooklyn Bridge. 1939. JOSEPH STELLA.

Baptism in Kansas. 1928. JOHN STEUART CURRY.

As the land has been diverse, so have the people who have lived on it. All types in all kinds of occupations have been subjects of the American artist. More than anything else, painters, like the ones on these pages, have tried to express the difference and the sameness in the American experience. At times this has made the ugly seem to predominate, but it has also given a dignity to the commonplace: Eugene Speicher's blacksmith at the far right has an Olympian strength about him. John Steuart Curry has put spirituality into his depiction of the simple country baptism above. Franklin C. Watkins' circus fire-eater at the right is a Prometheus reborn.

The Fire-Eater. 1933–34. FRANKLIN C. WATKINS.

1230

Red Moore, Blacksmith. 1935. EUGENE SPEICHER.

Swing Low, Sweet Chariot. 1939. JOHN MCCRADY.

Jane Reed and Dora Hunt. 1941. CLARENCE CARTER.

Tattoo and Haircut. 1932. REGINALD MARSH.

Here are three gentle, almost affectionate treatments of humble subjects. John McCrady softens the scene of death by showing the mythical chariot swinging low over the Southern cabin. Clarence Carter puts humor into his two angular Midwestern countrywomen gleaning coal fallen from passing trains. Reginald Marsh clearly has compassion for his Bowery derelicts.

OVERLEAF: These four paintings illustrate four degrees of abstraction—the first only slightly removed from representation, the last stopping well short of abandoning all suggestion of recognizable subject matter. The approaches of Hopper and Sheeler have much in common, as have those of Marin and Davis. All get their emphasis by simplifying details or leaving them out.

1233

Gas. 1940. EDWARD HOPPER.

American Landscape. 1930. CHARLES SHEELER.

Storm Over Taos. 1930. JOHN MARIN.

Bass Rocks No. 1. 1939. STUART DAVIS.

Martial Memory. 1941. PHILIP GUSTON.

American art in the period treated in this portfolio was not all quiet in mood. Many paint-ers, like William Gropper, long a radical cartoonist, commented bitterly on American insti-tutions. Others, like Fletcher Martin, were satisfied to capture action-filled situations. And still others, like Philip Guston, tried to convey a forceful meaning through symbolism.

Trouble in Frisco. 1938. FLETCHER MARTIN

The Senate. 1935. WILLIAM GROPPER

CHAPTER 42

RELIEF AND REFORM

The first three months of Franklin D. Roosevelt's administration was a period of new directions, innovation, and experimentation, formulated largely by his "brain trust." This corps of intellectual advisers included such men as Raymond Moley, recruited from Columbia University, where he had been a professor of public law; Rexford G. Tugwell, from an economics professorship at Columbia; and Adolf A. Berle, Jr., who advised part time while teaching (also at Columbia) and practicing law. Those who approved the New Deal's flood of novel remedies cheered; those who were doubtful waited to see, sharpening their arrows of outrage.

Within a year, "pump-priming" efforts showed results but gave no indication as to whether the American economy was making a genuine recovery or merely responding temporarily. All that was sure was that things were happening, and that there was spotty improvement. By 1934,

Low wheat prices in 1932 were ruinous to farmers, especially ones using old-fashioned methods, like the two scything their harvest in this painting by Thomas Hart Benton.

Southern farmers had enough ready cash to double the volume of their business with mail-order houses. They were replacing worn-out machinery and buying enough other items to increase Southern retail figures generally by as much as 60%. Meanwhile, the nation's wheat growers had responded to the Agricultural Adjustment Administration's program, removing some 8,000,000 acres of wheat land from production. About 555,000, or 80%, of the growers were signed up for the crop curtailments. The 1932–33 average price of wheat was slightly over 38¢ a bushel; the 1933–34 average exceeded 74¢. New Dealers attributed the healthy price increase to AAA action. Doubters pointed out that droughts had made crops poorer and thus prices higher.

Any such organization of agriculture was bound to bring criticism. Part of it stemmed from the precipitous way in which the Department of Agriculture assaulted the surplus problem. In the spring of 1933, Secretary of Agriculture Henry A. Wallace noted that the nation faced a glut of pork, and accordingly he sought ways to reduce the pig crop.

In 1933, Henry A. Wallace became Secretary of Agriculture, holding the same cabinet post his father had held under Harding.

As the new agricultural program had a late start that year, he saw no alternative but to order the slaughtering of newborn pigs, to keep them from coming to market. Although they were not being raised as pets, and were destined ultimately for food (some of it conceivably for families tired of a diet largely of rice and beans and potatoes), there was something repugnant to the American mind in making fertilizer out of them. Similarly, by the time the New Deal got under way that spring, it was obvious that there would be a large cotton crop. Again Wallace asked reduction and urged farmers to plow under a percentage of the 10,000,000 acres already planted. This, too, caused an uproar. Denis Brogan, in his *Era of*

Franklin D. Roosevelt, recounts how one farmer avoided the unhappiness of plowing under his own cotton crop by getting his neighbor to do it— while he plowed under his neighbor's crop. The result of the AAA measures, of course, was a rise in the price of both pork and cotton, but the fate of the "poor little pigs" left its mark upon the American conscience, and Wallace never heard the last of his mass-assassination order.

Courtroom counterattacks

If the farmers approved the major agricultural legislation, the Supreme Court did not. The first Agricultural Adjustment Act died under the judicial ax in January, 1936, when the court invalidated it on the ground that the processing tax was unconstitutional. The Roosevelt administration, however, had committed itself to agricultural relief, and it was not willing to give up. A month after the court decision, Congress passed the Soil Conservation and Domestic Allotment Act, which had much the same provisions as the former act, except that benefit payments came directly from the federal treasury, not through any special form of taxation. Armed with $500,000,000, Henry Wallace set forth to operate the "constitutional AAA." The farmers generally applauded Roosevelt's action; it was not among them that condemnation of "that man" was heard.

Businessmen, who had earlier flocked to the Blue Eagle's nest, took

Ten years before Adolf Dehn painted Beauty Is Where You Find It *in 1943, pigs were fewer in barnyards. Many were killed when newborn, to keep the pork price up.*

a different view. Unlike the farmers, they quickly tired of the partnership with government. Their initial delight at being able to fix prices through the "codes of competition" was vastly lessened by the required concessions to the laboring force. By late 1934 and early 1935, complaints against the National Recovery Administration had risen to a crescendo.

From the outset, there was some speculation as to the constitutionality of so widespread a change in American economic life. As the economy was in trouble and businessmen were happy to have some kind of relief, there was no immediate move to test the legitimacy of General Johnson's Blue Eagle in the courts. But during 1934 and 1935, as business

improved and there was a general price rise, merchants and manufacturers began to regain their confidence and became restive under the controls they had imposed on themselves by joining the NRA. When the government discovered the violators among those supposedly adhering to the NRA codes, it cracked down amid howls of "socialism." Actually, the NRA was something of a disappointment, even to its originators. It was an enormous task to formulate all the codes needed, and the work was done with the greatest haste. The result was inequities and confusion. Small firms charged that larger organizations received preferential treatment. Labor leaders complained about low wages. Consumers were unhappy

1241

Working under a grant from the WPA Federal Arts Project, Louis Ross (center) and two assistants paint a mural for the WPA Building at the 1939 World's Fair.

because of inflationary prices. The main trouble appeared to lie in the lack of uniformity in the codes. Some were highly complicated, while others were brief and general, subject to all kinds of interpretation. Many a small businessman, already burdened with details, was bewildered by the complexity of the regulations imposed on him. In May, 1935, the Supreme Court ended it all by declaring unconstitutional, in *Schechter Poultry Corp. vs. U.S.,* the National Industrial Recovery Act, under which NRA was created. The court held that Congress had overstepped itself in delegating so much power to the President in this instance and by abusing its own power over interstate commerce.

The Second New Deal

Although two of Roosevelt's major recovery programs suffered setbacks, the pace of new legislation did not slacken. The mid-term elections of November, 1934, contrary to the usual pattern of losses for the party in power, actually added nine House and nine Senate seats to the large Democratic majorities. With this encouragement, Roosevelt, in his annual message to Congress in January, 1935, outlined a program that included as many reform as recovery elements. He talked of financial security against old age, unemployment, and sickness; of better use of the country's resources generally as a means of improving the standard of living; of better housing and elimination of the worst housing by slum-clearance projects. From this period in Roosevelt's administration until domestic economic and social preoccupations were dwarfed by the urgencies of World War II, the New Deal's emphasis moved away from emergency depression measures typical of the Hundred Days toward long-range social legislation. For this reason, it is often referred to as the Second New Deal.

One major piece of relief legislation was yet to come, however. On April 8, 1935, Congress approved a program establishing the Works Progress Administration (WPA), which before its dissolution eight years later was to spend $11,000,000,000, mostly on wages and salaries for some 8,500,000 people. In conjunction with other government agencies in many cases, the WPA built many public buildings, bridges, airports, and parks that today are still important to their communities throughout the country. The main part of this work involved manual labor—"leaf-raking," in the word of its critics—but some of the WPA's best-known projects were cultural, with the government financing writers, artists, actors, and musicians.

One of the major pieces of social-reform legislation of the Second New Deal was the Social Security Act, passed on August 14, 1935. It provided for unemployment compensation and old-age insurance, with self-financing funds for payments to those no longer able to work. A clear distinction was made between the social security funds and the general tax revenues.

The latter became the subject of heated controversy in the summer of 1935 when Roosevelt proposed the use of taxes "to prevent an unjust con-

The strongly anti-Roosevelt Liberty League was formed in 1934 to combat socialism. Wealthy families like the du Ponts financed it; Democrats like Al Smith supported it.

centration of wealth and economic power." Congress responded with a graduated tax on corporate income, an excess-profits tax, and a steeply graded tax on top-bracket personal incomes. The measures were aimed not so much at raising revenue as at putting a brake on economic enlargement, and as such were a reversal of the philosophy of the NRA, with its emphasis on big industrial units. The final tax bill that was signed by Roosevelt on August 31 was not sig-

Uncle Sam watches Henry Wallace balance on his Agricultural Adjustment Administration. The Supreme Court toppled it in 1936.

nificant in terms of its immediate effect, having been watered down by Congress, but its social intent brought it considerable attention, including both praise and bitter denunciation.

The opposition

By 1935, Roosevelt-haters became a power to be reckoned with. The fighting core of this group was the Liberty League, formed in 1934 to counter "inroads of socialism." The du Ponts and other wealthy families provided the money to support the league, while Democrats such as the now disgruntled Alfred E. Smith and his friend ex-Governor Joseph B. Ely of Massachusetts attacked Roosevelt from within the Democratic Party.

Several prominent Republicans were considered as candidates to unseat Roosevelt in the 1936 election— Herbert Hoover; Senator William E. Borah of Idaho; Senator Arthur H. Vandenberg of Michigan; Colonel Frank Knox, Chicago newspaper publisher; and Governor Alfred M. Landon of Kansas. Landon won the nomination chiefly because of his record in his home state, where he had balanced the budget in difficult times. Another reason was his acceptance by liberal Republicans, who remembered his early Progressive role in the election of 1912. Landon's personality was totally unlike Roosevelt's; the Republicans hoped the public was tired enough of the President's exuberance to elect a quiet and more conservative man. They were

The sign shows that this school is one of 34,000 Public Works Administration projects that the government began in 1934 for a total cost of $4,250,000,000.

wrong. The nation had lost none of its willingness to go along with the experimenters in Washington. Signs of depression were still at hand. When the votes were in, Landon had only two states on his side, giving him only eight electoral votes. (Those Republican citadels gave birth to a play on an old election adage. "As goes Maine, so goes Vermont," Democratic wags observed.) Roosevelt captured 523 of the electoral votes. The popular vote was 27,751,612 to 16,681,913.

By the time Franklin Roosevelt was sworn in for his second term, the country was awaiting his counterattack on an opponent of the New Deal that was likely to be far more formidable than either the Liberty League or the Republicans—the Supreme Court. On February 5, 1937, he made his move. He recommended to Congress a reorganization of the entire federal judicial system. Charging that the existing court system was antiquated and incapable of performing an increasing number of duties, he proposed that if any federal judge did not retire at 70, the optional age, another judge should be appointed to assist him. As applied to the Supreme Court of the "Nine Old Men," the plan would have allowed Roosevelt to appoint enough additional justices to form the liberal majority he wanted for approval of his legislation.

Almost at once there were widespread charges of "court-packing." A number of conservative Democrats

Always ready to put on a show, New York's Mayor Fiorello H. La Guardia played store clerk to demonstrate the Food Stamp Plan.

joined the chorus, making more evident some of the divisions already in the party. About the time the uproar reached its climax, the court took a hand. In two decisions in the spring of 1937, it seemed to come around to more of a pro-New Deal position.

By June, it appeared that the court had "reformed" to such a degree that the Senate Judiciary Committee found no need to put the reorganization bill before Congress. Roosevelt had lost the battle in not getting support for his legislation, but claimed he had won the war in finding a court amen-able to his programs. (For more details, see *Roosevelt vs. the Supreme Court* at the end of this volume.)

The second term

In February, 1938, the New Deal launched a new and third AAA. The second one (1936) had provided financial aid to a large number of farmers through land rentals, but it did not deal effectively with surpluses—a problem that was getting worse rather than better. Although the act of 1938 again stressed conservation and continued the program of benefit payments, it incorporated a new provision known as the "ever-normal granary." To keep the national agricultural reserves high enough to prevent shortages in the event of a crop failure, yet discourage dumping on the market, it was now made possible for the individual farmer to store his crop and to borrow up to 75% of the parity price. Thus the farmer could get enough cash to pay his bills and provide for his family while he waited for a more favorable market. The law had the effect of putting a floor under agricultural prices.

Still another method of controlling surpluses was tried in 1939. Any family on relief buying between $1 and $1.50 worth of orange stamps—good in trade at any grocer's—received free 50¢ worth of blue stamps, which could be exchanged for any food products the government had declared surplus. The grocer, in turn, received cash from the government for all the stamps he took in. The experiment started in Rochester, New York, and within two years it had spread to 150 large cities. The outbreak of World War II ended the need for this means of surplus reduction. Almost overnight, Americans were using a new kind of stamp—ration stamps—to buy some of their groceries. The surpluses had given way to shortages.

Another primary concern of Roosevelt's second term was labor legislation. When the NRA was invalidated in 1935, businessmen approved, but labor protested that its gains would be wiped out. The administration and Congress answered with the Wagner-Connery Act, in July, 1935. It restored some NRA guarantees to labor: The right to bargain collectively was assured, and manufacturers were warned not to try to influence any labor union and not to discriminate against employees. The National Labor Relations Board, created by the act, proved to be an effective agency. By the end of 1939, it had ordered the breakup of 340 company unions, despite the opposition of the National Association of Manufacturers, which charged the NLRB with being prolabor.

To restore guaranteed minimum wages and maximum hours, also envisioned in the NRA, the administration steered through Congress the Fair Labor Standards Act of 1938. The law applied to employees in interstate commerce or producing goods for interstate commerce—so loose a definition that farmers, seamen, and

F.P.G.

In the '30s, growers of grain and corn— even as good as this Vermont champion's— found themselves with practically no market.

domestics were exempted—and set legal limits to protect the beneficiaries. Hours were originally fixed at 44 a week, and wages were to be no lower that 25¢ an hour. Employers were required to pay time and a half for overtime, which considerably reduced an old practice of asking workers to perform extra duties. In most occupations, children under 16 were forbidden employment.

Roosevelt's reverses

Although New Dealers were encouraged by the results of many of their programs of economic rehabili-

Most Republicans and even some Democrats accused Roosevelt of royal ambitions when he said he would run for a third term.

tation, there were also disheartening setbacks. For example, the President was eager to extend the principle of the highly successful Tennessee Valley Authority to other sections of the country, but Congress was unenthusiastic. That vast project, authorized in May, 1933, brought 21 dams under government control and effected an economic revolution for a large part of the middle South. Railroad opposition, applied through Congress, kept Roosevelt from realizing his dream of a St. Lawrence waterway—a project that was to come about two decades later in a Republican regime.

Perhaps the most disheartening development of all was a sharp business recession in late 1937 and early 1938. There was a recovery—one that made up for most of the lost ground—but the downturn struck a damaging blow to the administration's prestige. An accelerated relief program was set in motion with greatly increased Works Progress Administration funds poured out to the unemployed. The Public Works Administration stepped up its efforts, erecting new public buildings, libraries, museums, and schools. The nation's business improved. Supporters of the New Deal gave the administration credit; its critics said the recovery merely proved that the administration could not maintain a satisfactory economic level without deficit spending.

There was also disappointment among the party's political leaders. No longer did the Democrats unquestioningly follow Roosevelt as they had in the first balmy days of the New Deal. After the 1936 election, there was a growing divergence of opinion among them over basic policies. The "court war" of 1937 helped bring into the open some of these differences as important Democrats took issue with the President. In the 1938 mid-term election, Roosevelt tried to purge some of the rebellious brothers by asking the voters to reject them in favor of more liberal candidates. He opposed the re-election of Senator Walter F. George in Georgia, and in Maryland he warred against Senator Millard E. Tydings. Both George and Tydings won by decisive margins, handing the President a hard slap for his efforts.

The New Deal: An afterview

Roosevelt's efforts to bolster the economy and to reinvigorate social planning shaped an epoch in the nation's history. His administration reexamined the functions of government, and put into practice earlier progressive notions that the federal government's role should be much broader than that of merely exercising police duties. In the narrowest sense, the New Deal was an immediate and drastic attempt to answer pressing economic and social problems, but behind it lay a desire to establish long-range reforms. In any fair attempt to assess Roosevelt's efforts, both must be taken into consideration.

The New Deal, often referred to as a revolution, was revolutionary only in that what it did was rapid. The attempted changes grew out of ideas long familiar to American reformers. Both labor and agriculture had tried for more than half a century to gain a larger part of the national income. Nineteenth-century Agrarians and early 20th-century Progressives had fought for many a change that came to pass after March, 1933. To conservative minds, these developments were both radical and dangerous, but before a decade had passed, a good many people who had feared such changes were obliged to admit that the innovations were here to stay. As time went on, the new departure appeared to be less a threat to tradition than was at first supposed.

When Roosevelt came to office, the nation was faced by an agri-

The Seattle Times *summarized F.D.R.'s worsening relations with a recalcitrant Congress, which was beginning to rebel, in 1940, against his continuing domination.*

cultural problem that was still serious several decades later. Critics say his attempts to solve it failed, and they have some justification. Any failure was not, however, from lack of effort. The New Dealers attacked the agricultural depression with sincerity, vigor, and boldness. They tried to save from further disintegration and decay a sector upon which much of the nation's economic health depended. Nearly 6,000,000 farmers cooperated in the AAA program; 100,000 farm committeemen in 3,000 communities lent a hand in administering it. The fruit of their effort—admittedly aided by nature—was a steady rise in farm income from $5,000,000,000 in 1933 to $9,000,000,000 in 1940. The big weakness of the program was that its support had to come from public funds. In six years, the government handed out more than $3,000,000,000 for farm aid. Much more would be spent during the Truman and Eisenhower administrations. The problem that defied solution was one of continuing surpluses and failure to recover lost foreign markets. There is proof that the farmer's situation improved between 1933 and the outbreak of World War II, but there is also question whether the cost and the long-range commitments to ever more appropriations was not too high a price to pay. The argument was to continue long after Roosevelt's death.

It is even harder to evaluate the contribution of the New Deal to an improvement in economic conditions.

Certainly the NRA and the subsequent Wagner-Connery Act were a boon to labor. The government also gave aid to segments of business. It enlarged the RFC originated in the Hoover administration, lent assistance through the Export-Import Bank, subsidized shipping, provided new business opportunities with its federal housing program and its public works program, and assisted some of the utility companies through the Rural Electrification Administration. Businessmen were critical of the government's attempts to enter into a partnership with them in the NRA, but they were glad to receive help in the earliest days of that agency. They criticized the New Deal's efforts to "spend its way to prosperity," but they were happy to find new orders for their products in the various spending programs. For both industry and agriculture, World War II intervened before any major government plan could fairly be labeled either a great success or a dismal failure.

By January, 1939, Roosevelt was ready to announce the conclusion of his reform efforts under the New Deal. He told Congress that he wanted no more than a continuation of deficit spending until economic recovery was assured. He asked for no new reform legislation. By now, the President was deeply concerned about the power of totalitarian governments abroad and the threat they posed to international peace. Before that year was out, a new World War would be under way.

THE TATTOOED MAN

A Vanity Fair *cartoonist mocks the many New Deal programs, whose initials he sees as being tatooed on an unhappy Uncle Sam by Roosevelt's "brain trust."*

World conditions, which had been a contributing factor to the depression, would revitalize the American economy at a terrible price. And with this resurgence would come an end to further innovations in Roosevelt's unprecedented domestic policies. The New Deal, absorbed into the economics and politics of the country, had, in effect, come to an end.

MAIN TEXT CONTINUES IN VOLUME 15

F.D.R. vs. the Supreme Court

A SPECIAL CONTRIBUTION BY
MERLO J. PUSEY

After several decisions against the New Deal, F.D.R. decided to pack the Supreme Court with justices who would support him. He failed, but the court was never the same again.

The great struggle between the President and the Supreme Court in 1937 deeply stirred the nation because it brought Franklin D. Roosevelt's crusade against depression into collision with one of our most hallowed traditions.

In the first phase of the struggle, beginning in 1935, the court invalidated a large part of the New Deal, thereby incurring the wrath of the country and the White House. In the second phase, two years later, Roosevelt moved against the court more boldly than any other President had ever done. Public opinion then swung to the defense of the court, and F. D. R. suffered the most humiliating defeat of his career. Yet the final outcome was a victory for liberal interpretation of the Constitution as well as for independence of the judiciary.

To understand the intensity of the struggle, it must be remembered that in the middle '30s the country was still trying to climb out of the depression. In 1933, Roosevelt had come

The Supreme Court Building, designed by Cass Gilbert and completed in 1935, became the scene for the battle between Roosevelt and the court.

to power with the economy thoroughly demoralized. He had ushered in an almost revolutionary concept of government stewardship over the national economy. With the cooperation of a frightened Congress, he had devaluated the dollar and placed industry under a system of codes and agriculture under production quotas. He had created various other new instruments of power, initiated sweeping social reforms, and given organized labor the greatest impetus it had ever experienced.

The President's courage and industry were contagious. While the people applauded, Congress enacted almost every bill that the White House brain trust produced. Some of this recovery legislation has become a distinctive part of our national heritage. But many of the early emergency bills were experimental and poorly drafted. The men around the President realized that some of their ventures could scarcely be reconciled with the Constitution as it was then interpreted by the Supreme Court. But in their haste they passed lightly over this problem. A new era was dawning. Its methods and objectives could not be judged by the outmoded criteria. Many of the New Dealers concluded that, in any event, the Supreme Court would not dare to upset statutes on which the nation's recovery seemed to depend.

This illusion was shattered in 1935, when Chief Justice Charles Evans Hughes, writing on behalf of a unanimous court, invalidated the National Industrial Recovery Act. The court found the NIRA wanting on two counts: First, Congress had delegated extensive lawmaking powers to trade organizations acting with the approval of the President; second, it had swept under federal control wholly local activities only remotely related to the interstate commerce that Congress is authorized to regulate.

On the same Black Monday, the court unanimously struck down the Frazier-Lemke Act for relief of farm debtors, with Justice Louis D. Brandeis writing the opinion, and reversed the President's dismissal of William E. Humphrey from the quasi-judicial Federal Trade Commission.

In most of the early New Deal cases, the court had been unanimous, but as it moved on to more controversial issues, its longstanding internal schism was much in evidence. On the conservative side, Justices Willis Van Devanter, Pierce Butler, George Sutherland, and James C. McReynolds nearly always stood together. To them, any innovation was likely to appear as an unconstitutional seizure of power. The liberal wing, consisting of Justices Brandeis, Harlan F. Stone, and Benjamin N. Cardozo, was more inclined to give Congress a free rein unless it had flagrantly over-reached its power. Chief Justice Hughes occupied a middle ground, and Justice Owen J. Roberts often stood with him. For the New Deal, the result was fluctuation between reverses and narrow victories.

With Stone, Brandeis, and Cardozo dissenting, the four conservative justices— and sometimes Hughes and Roberts—invalidated a number of New Deal measures. The Agricultural Adjustment Act, the Municipal Bankruptcy Act, and the Guffey Act—designed to rescue the ailing coal industry—were all held unconstitutional. Finally, a majority of five released a legal block-buster by striking down New York State's minimum-wage law for women. Coming on the heels of many decisions rejecting the extension of federal power over the economy, this restriction of state power seemed to indicate that no government could legally cope with the grave problems of the depression. The court's extreme standpattism raised an outcry throughout the land. Dissenting opinions by Hughes and Stone, in which Brandeis and Cardozo joined, pointedly disclosed the alarm felt within the court itself over this reactionary trend.

The white-bearded Chief Justice, whose liberal instincts were neatly blended with a high regard for traditional constitutionalism, was almost as much concerned over this turn of events as was the President. Both brooded on how to save the country from the consequences of static legalism. But while Hughes thought in terms of correcting loosely drawn legislation and interpreting the basic law more liberally, Roosevelt turned toward more drastic measures.

Soon after the NIRA decision in 1935, F. D. R. had put his Attorney General, Homer Cummings, to work on what the President called the "court problem." But no conclusions were drawn, and the issue was astutely avoided in the 1936 Presidential campaign, except for a pledge in the Democratic platform that the problems of the day would be met in a constitutional manner. Republican charges that the President, if re-elected, would resort to the "tyranny" of court-packing met with impassioned Democratic denials.

Once Roosevelt's towering victory over Governor Alfred M. Landon was achieved, however, he moved against the court with supreme confidence. Cummings came up with the idea of naming new judges to replace the aged men on the bench. The fact that Justice McReynolds, when he had been Attorney General in 1913, had advanced such a plan for driving overage judges of the lower courts into retirement made this approach irresistible. To the President's delight, Cummings shrewdly camouflaged the scheme in the trimmings of judicial reform. With the aid of a few trusted lieutenants, he drafted a bill and a Presidential message to Congress.

There was no discussion of the bill with the cabinet, Congressional leaders, or members of the court. F. D. R. gave his annual dinner for the judiciary without breathing a word of his secret to the judges. Two days later, he disclosed the contents of his message to an incredulous group of cabinet and Congressional leaders a few minutes before he

Nine Old Men *was the title of this* New Masses *cartoon of the Supreme Court published in 1937. The members of the court were (left to right) Owen J. Roberts, Pierce Butler, Louis D. Brandeis, Willis Van Devanter, Chief Justice Charles Evans Hughes, James C. McReynolds, George Sutherland, Harlan Fiske Stone, and Benjamin N. Cardozo.*

jubilantly explained it to the surprised press.

The President represented his bill as a reform aimed at correcting injustice and relieving the court of congestion. His implication was that aged justices on the Supreme Court bench were rejecting an excessive number of petitions for review—a charge that almost every lawyer knew to be false. Although he called for a "persistent infusion of new blood" into the judiciary, there was only a vague hint of the bill's real purpose.

The heart of the bill was the provision giving the President authority to name an additional federal judge for every incumbent who had served 10 years and not resigned within six months after reaching the age of 70. As six members of the Supreme Court had passed that age limit, F. D. R. could immedi-

ately have appointed six new justices. If Chief Justice Hughes and his five aged associates had chosen to remain, the membership of the court would have been enlarged from 9 to 15.

Legislators gasped over the boldness of the plan, yet many of them gave it immediate support. Others who dared to speak out against it assumed their opposition would be futile. Senator Carter Glass summed up his despair by exclaiming, "Why, if the President asked Congress to commit suicide tomorrow, they'd do it!"

The impact on the justices varied. Roberts, the youngest, decided to resign if the measure were passed. Hughes, then 74, told his intimates, "If they want me to preside over a convention, I can do it." Brandeis, the eldest of the so-called Nine Old Men and one of the greatest liberals who ever sat on the Supreme

Court bench, was cut to the quick by the President's indiscriminate assault upon age. Without exception, the justices were hostile to the scheme.

The first jolt that the bill sustained was a wave of public reaction against the deceptive trappings of reform in which F. D. R. and Cummings had tried to camouflage their assault upon the court. It placed the administration forces on the defensive from the very beginning.

A second severe jolt came when Senator Burton K. Wheeler read a letter from Chief Justice Hughes to the Senate Judiciary Committee, which was conducting hearings on the

A Los Angeles Times *cartoonist adapts the Biblical saying about drawing a camel through the eye of a needle for his pictorial comment on President Roosevelt's futile attempt to pull his court plan through the Senate.*

bill. With cool logic, Hughes showed that the Supreme Court was abreast of its work, that it was liberal in granting petitions for review, and that an increase in the size of the court would impair its efficiency. "There would be more judges to hear," he wrote, "more judges to confer, more judges to discuss, more judges to be convinced and to decide." Without touching on the policy question, Hughes left the President's arguments a shambles.

The Senate hearings produced a chorus of opposition to the bill from distinguished leaders in many walks of life. This stiffened the spines of many legislators who had been worried but silent. The Republicans wisely kept in the background and let opponents of the bill in the President's own party lead the fight.

Meanwhile, a ferment had been working within the court. Some two months before the President had disclosed his plan, the justices had brooded afresh over the constitutionality of state minimum-wage laws and decided that their previous conclusion in the New York case had been wrong. The State of Washington asked the court to uphold a state minimum-wage law similar to the New York statute it had invalidated. In December, 1936, the court voted 4 to 4 to uphold the State of Washington law and to reverse its previous decision.

Four votes were enough to let the challenged statute stand because it had come to the Supreme Court with the sanction of the State of Washington's highest tribunal behind it. Three affirmative votes came from Hughes, Brandeis, and Cardozo. The fourth was that of Justice Roberts, who had switched sides from his position in the New York case.

Hughes, however, was loath to have an issue of such importance disposed of by an even vote and decided to hold the Washington case until Justice Stone, who was ill, returned to the bench. About February 1, 1937, Stone joined in a complete reversal of the old precedents, but before the opinion could be written, the court found itself under threat of being packed.

Much has been written about this dramatic change of direction by the court, but actually the Washington case did not effect a clean break with the past. The court had upheld broad applications of state powers in several cases. Roberts followed the reasoning of these decisions instead of clinging to the older precedent. His recognition of error indicated that the court did not regard itself as infallible and therefore redounded to its credit.

Support for Roosevelt's judiciary bill further crumbled on April 12, when the court upheld the National Labor Relations Act in the fateful Jones & Laughlin Steel Corporation case. The opinion of Chief Justice Hughes was a sweeping confirmation of the power of Congress to regulate industrial relations having a direct impact on interstate commerce.

A few weeks later, the Senate Judiciary Committee rejected the President's ill-fated judiciary legislation, just before the newly consolidated majority of the court gave its blessing to the Social Security Acts. These events spelled out the administration's defeat. in no uncertain terms, but rear-guard fighting continued because of a strange set of circumstances.

In devising remedies for the court problem, no one had had the wit to offer the aged justices a reasonable chance to retire. Even before 1937, both Van Devanter and Sutherland had been eager to lay down their tasks, but Supreme Court justices could retire from active service only by resignation, and Congress was then free to reduce their compensation, as indeed it had done in the case of Justice Oliver Wendell Holmes. So the aged judges held on despite some infirmities.

After the court fight began, opponents of the President's bill rushed through Congress a liberalized retirement measure. Senator William E. Borah then persuaded his friend Justice Van Devanter to retire in order to make way for an appointment by Roosevelt, who up to this time had had no opportunity to name a Supreme Court justice. But instead of easing the predicament, this single vacancy threw the White House into near panic.

The President had offered the first available seat to Senator Joseph T. Robinson, a conservative Democratic wheelhorse who, despite

Roosevelt confers with Joseph T. Robinson, Senator from Arkansas, who as majority leader was directing the court fight in the Senate. Previously Robinson, although he was then 65, had been offered the first place to open in the court.

grave misgivings, was directing the fight for the judiciary bill as majority leader of the Senate. If the President failed to honor his well-known promise to Robinson, he would be left without a friend in the Senate. Fulfilling the promise would have turned the court fight into a grotesque hoax, for Robinson, at 65, was the antithesis of the new blood for which the Roosevelt men were clamoring. Caught in this dilemma, the President had to continue fighting for his bill as the only means of balancing the prospective Robinson appointment with those of younger and more liberal men.

Thus the fight went on and the unfortunate Joe Robinson was increasingly torn between his distrust of the bill and his ambition to become a justice of the Supreme Court. On July

14, 1937, his troubled heart failed under the strain; his death knell also signaled the end for the judiciary bill. Shortly after Senator Robinson's funeral, the Senate formally buried the infamous measure by recommitting it to the Judiciary Committee.

Even this did not bring down the final curtain. F. D. R. struck back by naming as a successor to Justice Van Devanter one of his most ardent supporters in the court fight—a man who would be anathema to his foes in the Senate and who would nevertheless be in a position to command confirmation—Senator Hugo L. Black of Alabama. Shortly after his confirmation, disclosure that Black had once been a member of the Ku Klux Klan brought a fresh public clamor and intensified the bitterness of the whole affair.

Can this strange chapter in our history be regarded as an essential part of the process by which the Constitution has been modernized? Was President Roosevelt right in asserting that he had lost a battle and won a war? Since 1937, undoubtedly, the Supreme Court has in many instances taken a broader view of the powers of Congress. But this came about by an evolutionary process as different from court-packing as is an election from a *coup d'état.*

The chief reason that judicial decisions invalidating acts of Congress began to subside after 1937 was that Congress thereafter exercised greater care in casting its statutes. The reckless draftsmanship of the emergency period was eliminated. Sweeping delegations of power were avoided. Having fought a terrific battle to save the court from domination by the executive, Congress was especially eager to avoid legislation that might precipitate another showdown.

More important than anything else in the evolution of constitutional doctrine since 1937 has been the changed personnel of the Supreme Court. Before F. D. R.'s death in 1945, he had named seven of the nine members of the court and had elevated Stone to the chief justiceship.

The new justices went much further than the Hughes court had done in amplifying federal powers, and in general the country has welcomed these new interpretations.

If Roosevelt had sponsored a reasonable retirement bill for members of the Supreme Court in 1937, the evolutionary process would have been hastened and this entire chapter in our history could have been avoided. The chief difficulty seems to have been that after his triumphal re-election in 1936, the President was riding too high to deal with the court with the moderation and restraint that should guide the relations of one coordinate branch of government to another. He chose a method that might indeed have lifted restraints from Congress and the administration, but it would also have imperiled our constitutional system, the central genius of which is its system of checks and balances.

The justices who piloted the court through this difficult period won a double victory. The net effect of the 1935-37 ferment was to confirm their insistence that justices must take into account changed conditions as well as past legal precedents. After Justice Roberts abandoned his four conservative colleagues in the Washington minimum-wage case, they did not again control the court on any vital issue. The views that prevailed were those of Chief Justice Hughes and of Justices Brandeis, Stone, Cardozo, and Roberts.

The principle for which they struggled was continued independent judgment on the part of the court. They stood for a Constitution that marched forward—but not to tunes called by the White House or by a spate of new justices suddenly appointed for that purpose.

Contrary to Roosevelt's boast, it was these men who won both the "battle" and the "war" in 1937. A half-century after the notorious court-enlargement bill went down to defeat, it has scarcely a defender and remains one of the major errors of American statesmanship in the current century.

Merlo J. Pusey is the author of The Supreme Court *and of the authorized biography of Chief Justice Charles Evans Hughes, for which he received the Pulitzer and Bancroft Prizes in 1952.*

Volume 14
ENCYCLOPEDIC SECTION

The two-page reference guide below lists the entries by categories. The entries in this section supplement the subject matter covered in the text of this volume. A **cross-reference** (*see*) means that a separate entry appears elsewhere in this section. However, certain important persons and events mentioned here have individual entries in the Encyclopedic Section of another volume. Consult the Index in Volume 18.

AIR PIONEERS

Richard E. Byrd
Amelia Earhart
Harold Gatty

Charles A. Lindbergh
Billy Mitchell
Wiley Post

AMERICAN POLITICIANS AND STATESMEN

Hugo L. Black
Louis D. Brandeis
Pierce Butler
Hattie Caraway
Benjamin N. Cardozo
Anton Cermak
Homer Cummings
Joseph Ely
James A. Farley
John Nance Garner
Walter F. George
Carter Glass
Harold Ickes
Hugh S. Johnson
Frank B. Kellogg
Joseph P. Kennedy
Frank Knox

Fiorello La Guardia
Alfred M. Landon
Huey Long
James C. McReynolds
Andrew W. Mellon
Gerald P. Nye
Frances Perkins
Owen J. Roberts
Joseph T. Robinson
Eleanor Roosevelt
Franklin D. Roosevelt
Henry L. Stimson
Harlan F. Stone
George Sutherland
Millard E. Tydings
Arthur H. Vandenberg
Willis Van Devanter
Henry A. Wallace

BUSINESS AND INVENTION

George Washington Carver
Empire State Building
Joseph P. Kennedy

Ernest O. Lawrence
John L. Lewis
Andrew W. Mellon

DEPRESSION AND NEW DEAL

Adolph A. Berle, Jr.
Black Tuesday
Bonus Army
Bonus Expeditionary Force
Brain Trust
Thomas G. Corcoran
Great Depression

Liberty League
Raymond Moley
New Deal
Samuel Rosenman
Second New Deal
Francis E. Townsend
Rexford G. Tugwell

POLITICAL DEVELOPMENTS

Good-Neighbor Policy
Panay Incident

Twentieth Amendment
Twenty-first Amendment

THOUGHT AND CULTURE

Thomas Hart Benton
Erskine Caldwell
Al Capone
Walt Disney
James T. Farrell
First Scottsboro Case
George Gershwin
Bruno Richard Hauptmann
Edward Hopper
Bobby Jones

Ernest O. Lawrence
Aimee Semple McPherson
Reginald Marsh
Walter Millis
Margaret Mitchell
Eleanor Roosevelt
Scottsboro Boys
Billy Sunday
William Allen White
Grant Wood
Frank Lloyd Wright

B

BENTON, Thomas Hart (1889–1975). An American-scene painter, Benton was noted for his realistic murals of the South and Midwest. The artist, who was a grandnephew of Senator Thomas Hart Benton (1782–1858), was born in Missouri. After attending the Art Institute of Chicago (1906–1907), he continued his studies at the Academie Julian in Paris (1908–1911). In 1912, Benton returned to New York, where he became manager of an art gallery. During World War I, he served in the navy as a draftsman. In 1926, Benton accepted a teaching position at the Art Students League in New York City. He taught, painted, and traveled throughout America during the next decade. His first important mural was painted in 1931 for the New School for Social Research in New York. A realistic presentation of contemporary American scenes, it is characteristic of Benton in style and subject. His murals usually portray ordinary people of the Midwest and South in a graphic, dynamic style (*see p. 1238*). Believing that murals should be three-dimensional, Benton made his figures round and plastic, whether he was working in oil, tempera, or watercolor. In 1932, the painter executed the murals for the library in the old Whitney Museum of American Art in New York. They are now located in the New Britain Art Museum in Connecticut. The following year, he painted a historical mural for the Indiana exhibit at the Century of Progress Exposition in Chicago. From 1935 to 1941, Benton served as head of the painting department at the Kansas City Art Institute. He has also lectured at various colleges and universities. During the 1950s, he illustrated books and executed paintings on commission for use as advertising material. Benton's

Thomas Hart Benton

autobiography, *An Artist in America,* was published in 1937.

BERLE, Adolph A., Jr. *See* **Brain Trust.**

BLACK, Hugo LaFayette (1886-1971). One of the most controversial Associate Justices in the history of the Supreme Court, Black had consistently defended the freedoms guaranteed in the Bill of Rights and espoused a liberal interpretation of the Constitution. Born in Harlan, Alabama, Black attended public schools and was awarded a law degree from the University of Alabama in 1906. He established a law practice at Birmingham, where he held several local offices before enlisting in the army during World War I. Discharged in 1919, Black resumed his law career and earned a reputation for skillfully defending unions and for winning large settlements for clients in injury suits. Seeking potential political contacts, Black in 1923 joined the Birmingham branch of the Ku Klux Klan. He left it two years later when he announced his candidacy for the United States Senate, to which he was elected in 1926 and again in 1932 for a full term. As a Senator, Black conducted Senate investigations into ship and airmail subsidies and lobbyist activities in the early 1930s. He supported all the New Deal measures proposed by President **Franklin D. Roosevelt** (*see*) and was himself the sponsor of a wage-and-hour bill in 1937 to establish a scale of minimum wages and a 40-hour workweek. Black also acted as Roosevelt's spokesman in the Senate, when the President tried to "pack" the Supreme Court in 1936–1937. When **Willis Van Devanter** (*see*) resigned from the Supreme Court in 1937, Roosevelt nominated Black to replace him. This appointment met with heated opposition in the Senate from conservatives who described Black as "an intellectual leftist liberal from below the Mason and Dixon line." His nomination was confirmed by a vote of 63 to 16. When Black's Klan membership was disclosed shortly after he joined the Court, liberals called him a racist, and he admitted in a nationwide radio broadcast that he had briefly belonged to the Ku Klux Klan. Once on the Supreme Court, Black soon became an outspoken crusader for individual rights—particularly in the area of race relations. His judicial philosophy was derived from the conviction that individual rights had a "preferred position in the Constitution over economic rights," and that the freedoms in the Bill of Rights were "absolutes" and not subject to change. Since the early 1940s, Black's opinions, including many courageous dissents from the majority of the Court, have had a far-reaching effect on national policy. In *Everson vs. Board of Education* (1947), Black wrote the majority opinion that taxpayers' money could not be used to support parochial schools. Four years later, in *Dennis et al vs. United States,* Black dissented from a conviction, based on the Smith Act of 1940, that made it a crime to advocate the violent overthrow of the United States government. He held that mere talk does not present a "clear and

Hugo L. Black

present danger." In one of his most famous majority opinions—*Engel vs. Vitale* (1962)—Black ruled against the required reading of prayers in New York public schools. In another well-known case—*Wesbury vs. Sanders* (1964) —Black rendered the majority opinion that "as nearly as practicable, one man's vote in a Congressional election is to be worth as much as another's," which led to the reapportionment of Congressional districts throughout the nation on the basis of the so-called one-man, one-vote rule. He retired in September, 1971, at the age of 85.

BLACK TUESDAY. The stock-market crash that ushered in the Great Depression of the 1930s hit Wall Street hardest on Black Tuesday, October 29, 1929. Stock prices had been booming since 1924, but as early as 1927 President Calvin Coolidge (1872-1933) had been warned by an economic adviser that the market's basis was weak. No steps were taken to check the boom by either Coolidge or his successor, Herbert Hoover (1874-1964), who had been Coolidge's Secretary of Commerce. The crash that came in October, 1929, was worse than anyone had imagined (*see pp. 1175-1180*). The first serious drop occurred on October 24,

known as Black Thursday, when nearly 13,000,000 shares of stock were traded. That day, leading bankers pledged millions of dollars to bolster the market and were able to stave off a total collapse on the last two days of the trading week, Friday and Saturday. Before the stock exchanges reopened on Monday, Hoover reportedly remarked that "the fundamental business of the country ... is on a sound and prosperous basis." However, by Black Tuesday, prices had dropped drastically, and an avalanche of selling had left ticker tapes hours behind, so that brokers had no idea of the current prices of the stocks they were unloading. Although Black Tuesday was the most dramatic day of the stock-market collapse— nearly 16,500,000 shares were traded—it was by no means the last. However, its suddenness and devastating effect served to reveal the underlying instability of the nation's economy. As stock prices continued to fall, a total economic collapse occurred. Banks failed, factories closed, and millions of Americans lost their jobs. Hoover tried unsuccessfully to counteract the crash by announcing a tax cut in November, 1929, that was meant to increase purchasing power. He urged private industry to postpone wage reductions and maintain production levels. However, he was adamantly

against "any direct or indirect government dole." "Prosperity cannot be restored," he said, "by raids upon the public Treasury." Stock values finally hit bottom in September, 1932, when average prices were 87% below the highs of September, 1929. By then, the Depression was in full swing. The gross national product was down 40% from 1929, and the number of unemployed had reached 12,000,-000. Historians have found numerous causes for the crash: An uneven distribution of wealth led to excessive stock activity; too many investors were speculators who hoped to make a quick profit by buying and then selling as the market rose; the vast interconnection between banks caused the collapse to spread rapidly from bank to bank; overly complex, unsound corporate holding companies made it difficult or impossible to assess the real value of many stocks; and too many investors were buying on margin— with only 10% in cash behind their stock purchases. Underlying all these factors was a widespread, naive optimism within the American public, typified by an article written early in 1929 for the *Ladies' Home Journal* by financier John J. Raskob (1879-1950). Entitled "Everybody Ought to be Rich," the article showed that anyone who invested $15 a week could make $80,000 in 20 years.

STOCK PRICES SLUMP $14,000,000,000 IN NATION-WIDE STAMPEDE TO UNLOAD; BANKERS TO SUPPORT MARKET TODAY

Sixteen Leading Issues Down $2,893,520,108; *Tel. & Tel. and Steel Among Heaviest Losers*	**PREMIER ISSUES HARD HIT**
A shrinkage of $2,893,520,108 in the open market value of the shares of sixteen representative companies resulted from yesterday's sweeping decline on the New York Stock Exchange. American Telephone and Telegraph was the heaviest loser, $448,905,162 having been lopped off of its total value. United States	**Unexpected Torrent of Liquidation Again Rocks Markets.**

On the morning of Black Tuesday, the New York Times *headlined the previous day's slump. The efforts of the bankers failed and stock prices plunged lower.*

BONUS ARMY. During the height of the Depression in 1932, about 15,000 jobless World War I veterans marched to Washington, D. C., to demand that the government immediately pay them for their Adjusted Compensation (or "Bonus") Certificates, which had been issued by Congress in 1924 and were not redeemable until 1945. Mobilizing at Portland, Oregon, under the leadership of Walter W. Waters, a former sergeant, and adopting the motto "No panhandling, no drinking, no radicalism," the so-called Bonus Army began walking, hitchhiking, and riding on freight trains to the nation's capital. On the way, the veterans got into a skirmish with railroad officials in East St. Louis, Illinois, and were expelled from the state by the National Guard. Finally arriving in Washington in late May, the veterans camped in hastily built shacks and abandoned government buildings and vowed to remain until Congress authorized the cash redemption of their certificates. At first, President Herbert Hoover (1874–1964) wanted to drive the veterans away at gunpoint, as he had done to hunger protesters the previous winter, but the Washington chief of police, who was sympathetic toward the veterans, persuaded him to avoid violence. Although the Bonus Army maintained rigid discipline and drove Communist agitators from its ranks, the problems of inadequate food, shelter, and sanitation and the latent threat of disorder alarmed local authorities. When a proposed bill to grant the veterans $2,500,000,000 was defeated by the Senate on June 17, 1932, Hoover offered to pay their fare home, and most of the Bonus Army disbanded. However, about 2,000 veterans stayed and refused to evacuate when ordered to do so. After two policemen and two veterans were killed in a scuffle, the President, on July 28, 1932, called out the army to crush the

World War I veterans parade in Washington, D.C., to demand their bonuses.

resistance by force. The troops, led by General Douglas MacArthur (1880–1964), drove the veterans from their camps and public buildings with bayonets and tear gas, finally dispersing the remnants of the Bonus Army. In January, 1936, the bonus was paid over the veto of President **Franklin D. Roosevelt** (*see*).

BONUS EXPEDITIONARY FORCE. *See* **Bonus Army.**

BRAIN TRUST. Near the end of his term as governor of New York (1929–1933) and in his first years as President, **Franklin D. Roosevelt** (*see*) gathered about him a group of advisers who, because of their academic affiliations and reputations as intellectuals, came to be known as the Brain Trust. Among the most influential of these advisers were three Columbia University professors: Raymond Moley (1886–1975), a specialist in public law; Rexford G. Tugwell (1891–1979), an agricultural economist; and Adolph A. Berle, Jr. (1895–

1971), a financial expert. Other Brain Trusters whose political liberalism and expertise in economic and social problems had a significant impact on New Deal policies included attorney Samuel I. Rosenman (1896–1973), who was one of Roosevelt's chief speech writers; Harry L. Hopkins (1890–1946), a social-welfare administrator and head (1935–1938) of the Works Progress Administration; Frances Perkins (*see*), Roosevelt's Secretary of Labor (1933–1945) and the first woman to serve in a Presidential cabinet; and Thomas G. Corcoran (1900–1981) and Benjamin V. Cohen (1894–1983), two lawyers who were specialists in investment legislation. Many of these advisers were appointed to various governmental positions, while others served in an informal capacity. The Roosevelt advisory group was influential in drafting New Deal legislation during the President's first term. Afterward, it was gradually disbanded. The expression "Brain Trust," first applied to F.D.R.'s advisers by a New York *Times* reporter in 1932, was revived in the early 1960s to refer to the academic advisers recruited by President John F. Kennedy (1917–1963).

BRANDEIS, Louis Dembitz (1856–1941). From the time that he was labeled the people's attorney throughout his 23 years as an Associate Justice (1916–1939) of the Supreme Court, Brandeis was known as a champion of liberalism. Born in Louisville, Kentucky, Brandeis received his law degree from Harvard in 1877 and began practicing law in Boston in 1879. He soon established a reputation as a liberal. From 1900 to 1907, Brandeis served as counsel for the citizens of Boston in a lawsuit against the local public utilities and succeeded in preventing a rise in the cost of gas. Because he refused to be paid for his services, he was dubbed the people's attorney. Dealing increasingly with problems of social justice, Brandeis successfully fought for insurance- and railroad-rate reforms, as well as conservation and minimum-wage laws. Appearing before the Supreme Court in 1908 in a case concerning minimum hours for women workers, Brandeis supported his arguments by using what became known as the Brandeis Brief—that is, psychological, social, and economic information to convince the Court to uphold the legislation. This marked the first time that arguments other than legal precedents and generalizations were accepted by the Court as the basis for an appeal. During the Presidential campaign of 1912, Brandeis helped Woodrow Wilson (1856–1924) formulate his New Freedom policy, which emphasized the prevention of business monopolies. Four years later, over the opposition of those who objected to his liberal views and Jewish faith, Wilson appointed him to the Supreme Court. During his early years as an Associate Justice, Brandeis, along with Oliver Wendell Holmes (1841–1935), constantly dissented from the Court majority, which was generally conservative in its views. Late in the second administration of President **Franklin D. Roosevelt** (*see*), the Court grew more liberal, and the opinions of Brandeis, who was now frequently in the majority, were often cited to explain the Court's rulings. Retiring from the bench in 1939, Brandeis devoted his time to the American Zionist movement. As the first Jew to sit on the Supreme Court, Brandeis established a tradition for at least one Jew to serve on the nation's highest tribunal. This remained in effect until the resignation of Justice Abe Fortas (1910–1982) in 1969. In 1948, the first Jewish-endowed nonsectarian college was founded in Waltham, Massachusetts, and named Brandeis University in his honor.

BUTLER, Pierce (1866–1939). An Associate Justice of the Supreme Court from 1923 to 1939, Butler was a fierce conservative who adamantly opposed the New Deal policies and legislation of President **Franklin D. Roosevelt** (*see*). A native of Dakota County, Minnesota, Butler attended Carleton College, graduating in 1887. He was admitted to the Minnesota bar the following year and began a successful practice in St. Paul. A forceful speaker with a sure command of fact and legal argument, Butler specialized in railroad-rate cases, in which he became an acknowledged expert. Between 1913 and 1922, he was a consultant to both the American and Canadian governments on railroad law. His partnership—Butler, Mitchell, and Doherty—was one of the outstanding legal firms in the Northwest. Over the objections of organized labor and liberal Congressmen, Butler was appointed to the Supreme Court in 1922 by President Warren G. Harding (1865–1923). From the first, he opposed the centralization of power in both federal and state governments, and his opposition intensified with the coming of the New Deal in 1933. Butler voted against such legislation as minimum-wage laws, limitations on what employment agencies could charge, municipal zoning, and requirements that states provide blacks with the same educational services as whites. He also voted to strike down many New Deal measures for coping with the Depression, including the Agricultural Adjustment Act, the National Industrial Recovery Act, and the Municipal Bankruptcy Act (*see pp. 1253–1258*). The argumentative and immovable Butler dissented 73 times from the majority opinion of his fellow Justices during the New Deal years. He died before the Court came to be dominated by liberal sentiment during the latter part of Roosevelt's second term in office.

BYRD, Richard Evelyn (1888–1957). The intrepid leader of five exploratory expeditions to Antarctica, Byrd was the first man to fly over both the North and South Poles. The Virginia-born explorer graduated from Annapolis in 1912. During World War I, he was trained as a pilot in Pensacola, Florida, and later was stationed in Canada as head of the United States Navy's air forces there. In 1919, he was put in charge of the navigational preparations for the navy's first transatlantic flight. Byrd began his career as an explorer in 1925, when he was given command of the aviation unit attached to the Navy-MacMillan Arctic Expedition. The following year, he led a privately financed expedition to the Arctic. At that time, Byrd and his copilot, Floyd Bennett (1890–1928), flew 1,360 miles from Kings Bay, Spitsbergen, Norway, to the North Pole and back in a trimotored Fokker, becoming the first men to cross the North Pole. The historic flight earned both aviators the Medal of Honor. Byrd then turned his attention to Antarctica, where he was to make his greatest achieve-

Byrd returns to Spitsbergen after his historic flight across the North Pole in 1926.

ments. In 1928, he led his first expedition there, sailing south with two ships on a privately sponsored venture. After establishing a base named Little America on the Bay of Whales, the Byrd party discovered the Rockefeller Range and Marie Byrd Land. The following year, the explorer and three companions flew a three-engine Fokker from Little America 1,600 miles to the South Pole and back, thus becoming the first men to fly over the South Pole. Byrd was subsequently promoted to rear admiral and given a hero's reception upon his return to America (*see p. 1210*). He described the expedition in *Little America* (1930). The explorer led a second expedition to Antarctica in 1933. With Little America again the base camp, the Byrd party explored 200,000 square miles of the continent. At this time, the Ruppert Coast, the Rockefeller Plateau, and the Edsel Ford Range were charted. Byrd himself established an advance base 123 miles closer to the South Pole, where he wintered alone for five months in 1934. When his men came for him, he was nearly dead from carbon-monoxide poisoning from a faulty stove. Byrd recorded his solitary winter in *Alone* (1938). The explorer's third expedition to Antarctica, made in 1939, was the first to receive government back-

ing. Before its return in 1940, the Byrd party discovered five new mountain ranges, a peninsula, and several islands. Six years later, the explorer returned to the same area as commander of Operation Highjump, a naval expedition to map the continent. In 1955, Byrd led his fifth and last expedition to the Antarctic, Operation Deep Freeze I. Its purpose was to select and prepare American bases for the International Geophysical Year studies. He died two years later in Boston. His brother, Harry F. Byrd (1887–1866), was governor (1926–1930) of Virginia and a United States Senator (1933–1965).

C

CALDWELL, Erskine (1903–1987). A novelist and short-story writer, Caldwell wrote *Tobacco Road,* a book whose title became synonymous with Southern degeneration. The writer was born in Georgia and as a child lived throughout the South. He began his literary career writing short stories while a student at the University of Virginia in the 1920s. Caldwell interrupted his education to work in a store, play professional football, pick cotton, and sell "building lots in Alabama under three feet of water." After briefly attending the University of Pennsylvania, he

resumed his studies in Virginia. He again left college, about 1928, this time to join the staff of the Atlanta *Journal* as a reporter. A year later, he resigned from the newspaper and moved to Maine. During five years there, he wrote *Tobacco Road* (1932) and *God's Little Acre* (1933). *Tobacco Road,* the story of an impoverished farm family living on a back road in Georgia, was made into a play that opened in 1933 and ran for 3,182 performances, the sixth-longest-running drama in Broadway history. *God's Little Acre,* a similar portrait of Georgia mountain people, was released as a film in 1958. The explicit sex scenes in Caldwell's novels have often been the cause of obscenity charges against the author. In 1941, Caldwell went to Russia as a war correspondent. Married at the time to photographer Margaret Bourke-White (1906–1971) he collaborated with her on three books of nonfiction, *You Have Seen Their Faces* (1937), *North of the Danube* (1938), and *Say! Is This the U.S.A.?* (1941). After the war, Caldwell again wrote about the "po' whites" of his native Georgia in *A House in the Uplands* (1946), *The Sure Hand of God* (1947), and *This Very Earth* (1948). His other works include *A Lamp for Nightfall* (1952), *Love and Money* (1954), *Claudelle Inglish* (1959), *Jenny By Nature* (1961), and *Around About America* (1964). He is also known for his short stories, among them "Daughter" and "Kneel to the Rising Sun."

CAPONE, Alphonse ("Al") (1899–1947). The leading gangland chief of Chicago, Al Capone was a bootlegger, a dope peddler, a racketeer, a briber, an extortionist, and a popular hero to millions of Americans in the 1920s. Born in Naples, Italy, he grew up in a Brooklyn slum, where he acquired the nickname Scarface after being knifed in a gang fight. In 1920, he moved to Chicago to work for mobster Johnny Torrio as a bouncer in a brothel. By the end of 1921, he had become Torrio's chief assistant and gunman. Early in 1925, Torrio was shot and wounded by a rival gang. He transferred his business to Capone and sailed for Italy. Previously, Capone had set up his headquarters in Cicero, Illinois, by importing 200 gunmen from Chicago to fix the mayoral election. Capone traveled around in a $20,000, seven-ton armored car, wore a $50,000 diamond ring, and received fan mail from around the world for his open defiance of prohibition laws (*see p. 1212*). The Federal Bureau of Internal Revenue estimated his income for 1927 alone at $105,000,000. The five years that Capone ruled the Chicago area were punctuated by fierce gangland wars in which more than 500 thugs were killed. The wars reached a climax in the Valentine's Day Massacre of 1929, in which Capone had seven rival gangsters eliminated (*see p. 1154*). The event alarmed underworld chieftains and marked the end of Chicago's easy acceptance of gang rule. In May, 1929, Capone was arrested and sentenced to a year in prison for carrying a concealed weapon. He was released from prison in March, 1930, and returned to Chicago, but he found himself no longer welcome. In 1931, Capone was indicted for income-tax evasion. Federal agents refused his $4,000,000 bribe attempt, and he was convicted and sentenced to 11 years in prison. In ill health, Capone was released from Alcatraz in 1939 and spent his remaining years in Miami, Florida.

CARAWAY, Hattie Wyatt (1878–1950). A homespun housewife from Arkansas who had never seen a railroad until she was 24 years old, "Miss Hattie" was the first woman elected to the United

States Senate (*see p. 1214*). The Tennessee-born farm girl entered Dickson Normal College in 1892. Six years after she graduated in 1896, she married a young lawyer, Thaddeus H. Caraway (1871–1931), and settled in Lake City, Arkansas, where the couple had three children. In 1912, when Mr. Caraway was elected to the House of Representatives, the family moved to Washington, D. C. Eight years later, he was elected to the first of two terms in the Senate. When Caraway died in 1931, near the end of his second term, Governor Harvey Parnell (1880–1936) appointed his widow to fill out the unexpired term. Mrs. Caraway's first official statement on joining the Senate was, "The windows need washing." With the term about to expire in 1933, Senator **Huey Long** (*see*) of Louisiana suggested that she run for a full six-year term. Long advised her to change her colorful dresses for drab widow's garb and to stick to wearing only one hat while campaigning. Long then campaigned throughout Arkansas, urging the voters to send Miss Hattie back to the Senate. Defeating six other candidates, Mrs. Caraway became the first woman to be elected to the Senate. During her 13 years in it—she was reelected in 1938—Mrs. Caraway rarely made speeches or participated in debates, not having "the heart to take a minute away from the men. The poor dears love it so." During sessions, she often worked on crossword puzzles. She remarked at the end of one debate, "It's funny how they talk on after we've all made up our minds." Mrs. Caraway made little effort to be reelected in 1944 and was defeated by J. William Fulbright (born 1905). Although the first woman elected to the Senate, Mrs. Caraway was not the first woman to serve in it. That distinction belonged to 87-year-old Mrs. Rebecca L. Felton (1835–

1930) of Georgia, who served one day. She was appointed to the Senate on October 3, 1922, to fill out part of the unexpired term of Senator Thomas E. Watson (1856–1922). She was not sworn in, however, until November 21, and on the following day, **Walter F. George** (*see*), who had been chosen in a special election for Watson's seat earlier in the month, succeeded her when he was sworn in.

CARDOZO, Benjamin Nathan (1870–1938). As an Associate Justice of the United States Supreme Court during one of the most tempestuous periods in its history (*see pp. 1252–1258*), Cardozo, along with **Louis D. Brandeis** and **Harlan F. Stone** (*see both*), formed a "liberal minority" whose dissents eventually paved the way for a broad interpretation of federal powers. Cardozo was descended from a Sephardic Jewish family that had resided in New York City since colonial days. He was tutored by the author Horatio Alger (1834–1899) and graduated from Columbia in 1889. He earned his Master's degree there the following year. Although he did not receive a law degree, Cardozo passed the New York bar in 1891, and for the next 22 years practiced law, serving mainly as an attorney for other lawyers and as a referee in commercial cases. Elected to the New York supreme court in 1913, Cardozo remained

Benjamin N. Cardozo

a trial judge for only six weeks and then was temporarily appointed to the state court of appeals, to which he won a full 14-year term in 1917. He became chief judge in 1927, and dealing primarily with common-law cases, made the appellate court second in distinction only to the United States Supreme Court itself. Like Justice Oliver Wendell Holmes (1841–1935), Cardozo viewed the judicial process as a mixture of continuity and creativity, and he adapted past precedent in the light of social change. His philosophy of sociological jurisprudence was developed in three classic works—*The Nature of the Judicial Process* (1921), *The Growth of the Law* (1924), and *The Paradoxes of Legal Science* (1928). When Holmes resigned from the United States Supreme Court in 1932, the legal profession insisted that Cardozo be his successor. At first, President Herbert Hoover (1874–1964) was wary of naming a third New Yorker to the bench—Justices Stone and Charles Evans Hughes (1862–1948) were already from that state—or another Jew—as Brandeis was. However, Hoover finally agreed to appoint Cardozo to fill the vacancy. Regarding his role on the Supreme Court as that of "historian and prophet all in one," Cardozo applied his liberal philosophy to constitutional law. He urged the Court to "look beyond the particular to the universal, and shape [its] judgment in obedience to the fundamental interests of society." A supporter of **Franklin D. Roosevelt** (*see*) and the New Deal, Cardozo frequently dissented from the majority of the Court that nullified much of the President's legislative program. At the same time, however, he believed that the President's powers should conform to those prescribed in the Constitution. One of the most significant opinions Cardozo wrote was his majority ruling on the social-security cases

of 1937, in which he demonstrated that a federal act, designed to meet specific human needs at a particular moment in history, could be compatible with the abiding spirit of the Constitution. A heart attack and stroke limited Cardozo's term on the Court to a brief six years.

CARVER, George Washington (1864?–1943). Often called the Goober Wizard or the Columbus of the Soil, this black botanist revolutiónized agriculture in the South by teaching farmers principles of crop rotation and soil improvement. He also developed hundreds of uses for such easy-to-grow plants as the goober pea or

cultural science. In 1894, he became the first black student to graduate from the college, and he received a Master's degree there two years later. In 1896, Carver joined the faculty of Tuskegee Institute in Alabama, where he taught and served as director of agricultural research for the rest of his life. At the agricultural station established at Tuskegee to study ways of bettering the economic lot of black Americans, Carver conducted the research that brought him international renown. He discouraged the cultivation of cotton, which quickly exhausted the soil, and urged farmers to grow soil-enriching peanuts, soybeans, and sweet potatoes. To prevent a surplus of these food

Carver developed famous food by-products in his laboratory at Tuskegee Institute.

peanut, the pecan, and the sweet potato. Born into slavery near Diamond Grove, Missouri, Carver was raised by his former master, Moses Carver. About 1874, he set out on his own, working his way through elementary and high school. Entering Iowa State College in 1890, Carver studied agri-

crops, Carver developed in his laboratory about 300 synthetic products from peanuts, including milk, butter, coffee, flour, ink, and soap. He also devised more than 100 products from the sweet potato, including starch, vinegar, and molasses, and found about 60 new uses for the pecan.

Utilizing what would ordinarily be considered waste materials, Carver also made synthetic marble from wood shavings, paint pigments from Alabama clay, carpets from okra fibers, and fertilizer from swamp mud. He intended these inventions to benefit mankind and would not patent them or accept payment for their commercial use. After 1935, Carver was a government adviser for the Bureau of Plant Industry of the Department of Agriculture. In 1940, he gave his life savings of $33,000 to Tuskegee Institute. In 1953, 10 years after his death, the first federal monument to a black was erected on his grave at the plantation on which he was born.

CERMAK, Anton Joseph (1873–1933). The mayor of Chicago, Cermak was mortally wounded by an assassin who missed shooting President-elect **Franklin D. Roosevelt** (*see*) in February, 1933. Born near Prague, Czechoslovakia, Cermak had been brought as an infant to Illinois, where his father became a coal miner. After leaving public school at 16 for a series of low-paying jobs, Cermak became a self-employed peddler of waste wood. By the age of 35, he was a partner in a real-estate company and president of a bank and a building-and-loan association. His political career began in 1902, when he was elected as a Democrat to the first of three terms in the state legislature. In 1909, Cermak became a member of the city council. He served on it until 1922, when he was elected chairman of the County Board of Commissioners. As chairman (1922–1931), Cermak built an efficient political machine and rose to be head of Chicago's Democratic Party. He was elected mayor of the city in 1931. During the Democratic National Convention the following year, Cermak was able to swing Illinois' votes to Roosevelt. Cermak was in Miami,

Florida, to ask political favors for his city from the vacationing President-elect when the assassin struck. On February 15, 1933, Giuseppe Zangara (1900–1933)— a semiliterate, unemployed bricklayer who hated "all officials and everybody who is rich"—shot a volley of bullets at Roosevelt's open car as it stood in front of Bayfront Park, where Roosevelt had just addressed a crowd. Five persons, including Cermak, were wounded. Cermak died on March 6, 1933, two days after Roosevelt's inauguration. Zangara was tried and convicted twice—first on charges of assault and then, after Cermak's death, on charges of murder. He was executed on March 20, 1933, 33 days after the attack.

CORCORAN, Thomas G. *See* **Brain Trust.**

CUMMINGS, Homer Stille (1870–1956). As Attorney General of the United States under President **Franklin D. Roosevelt** (*see*) from 1933 to 1939, Cummings helped formulate Roosevelt's strategy for replacing aging conservative Justices on the Supreme Court with liberal appointees sympathetic to the policies of the New Deal (*see pp. 1252–1258*). A native of Chicago, Cummings attended Yale, graduating in 1891 and receiving his law degree two years later. After being admitted to the Connecticut bar in 1893, he practiced for most of his life in Stamford, where he served as the town's mayor (1900–1902 and 1904–1906). Cummings became known in politics during his 25 years (1900–1925) as a member of the Democratic National Committee and his brief term (1919–1920) as its chairman. At the Democratic National Convention in Chicago in 1932, Cummings was a floor leader in Roosevelt's successful bid for the party nomination. The following year, the new President

appointed him to the post of Attorney General after his original appointee, Thomas J. Walsh (1859–1933), died before he could take office. During his six years in office, Cummings, in addition to leading Roosevelt's campaign against the "Nine Old Men" on the Supreme Court, made many reforms in the federal prison system, sponsored a national conference on crime, strengthened the Federal Bureau of Investigation, and secured the passage of legislation extending federal jurisdiction in interstate criminal offenses. Cummings retired from the Justice Department in 1939 to return to his law practice in Stamford.

D

DISNEY, Walter Elias ("Walt") (1901–1966). Walt Disney was a film producer who pioneered in the development of animated cartoons and whose name became synonymous with children's entertainment projects. Raised on a Missouri farm, Disney studied at the Academy of Fine Arts in Chicago. During World War I, he drove an ambulance for the Red Cross in France. Disney worked as an advertising illustrator in Kansas City before moving to Hollywood in 1920. There, he began his career as a cartoonist, making *Alice Comedies* (1923–1926). The movies were made by individually filming a series of drawings that traced each movement. When the film was then projected, the illusion of movement was created. Disney created his first popular cartoon character, Oswald the Rabbit, in 1926. Two years later, he introduced the character of Mickey Mouse in *Steamboat Willie,* the first sound cartoon (*see p. 1211*). The popular mouse brought his creator immediate fame. That same year, Disney established his own company, Walt Disney Productions,

Walt Disney

Ltd., and began producing *Silly Symphonies,* the first color cartoons. His synchronization of music with pictures in this series further enhanced his reputation. Additional characters joined Mickey on the drawing board, among them Donald Duck, Pluto, and Goofy. In 1932, Disney released the first successful technicolor cartoon, *Trees and Flowers.* It was followed by *The Three Little Pigs* (1933), *The Tortoise and the Hare* (1934), and other cartoons. In 1938, Disney produced the first feature-length animated cartoon, *Snow White and the Seven Dwarfs,* for which 600 artists sketched 2,000,000 separate drawings. Two years later, he attempted to illustrate classical music with interpretive cartoons in *Fantasia.* Still experimenting, Disney employed variations in color to create an emotional effect in *Bambi* (1942). Disney interrupted his commercial career during World War II to produce animated films for propaganda use. A year after the war ended, he made *Song of the South* (1946), one of the first films to feature live actors and cartoon characters together. During the 1950s, the cartoonist ventured into the field of documentary film. *The Living Desert* (1953) was the first in a series of filmed nature studies. Disney,

who had won many Academy Awards, conceived and designed one of the largest amusement parks in the world, Disneyland, in Anaheim, California, which opened in 1955.

E

EARHART, Amelia (1898–1937). A pioneer in the field of aviation, Miss Earhart was the first woman to fly alone across the Atlantic Ocean and set other firsts as a solo pilot (*see p. 1214*). A native of Kansas, Miss Earhart volunteered as a nurse's aid in a Canadian military hospital during World War I, after which she became a teacher and social worker in Boston. While in California, she began learning to fly, and in 1920 she made her first solo flight. Eight years later, with pilot Wilmer Stutz and mechanic Louis Gordon, she became the first woman to cross the Atlantic in an airplane. In 1931, the attractive aviatrix married George Palmer Putnam (1887–1950), a New York publisher. On May 20, 1932—five years after **Charles Lindbergh** (*see*) made his nonstop solo flight from New York to Paris—Miss Earhart took off alone from Harbor Grace, Newfoundland, in an attempt to cross the Atlantic. Fourteen hours and 56 minutes later, her Lockheed Vega landed in a pasture in Londonderry, Ireland. It was the first solo transatlantic flight made by a woman. On January 11, 1935, she scored another first by being the first woman to fly from Hawaii to California, and on May 8 of that same year she flew nonstop from Mexico City to Newark, New Jersey. Two years later, Miss Earhart took off from Miami, Florida, with navigator Frederick J. Noonan for a 27,000-mile flight around the world. On one of the last legs of their journey, they left Lae, New Guinea, on July 1 for Howland Island in the Pacific. Early the next morning, Miss Earhart radioed that the plane's gasoline supply was running low. An hour later, she was cut off abruptly after reporting, "We are on line of position. . . ." Her Lockheed Electra never reached its destination. Despite an extensive search, the plane was never found and was assumed lost at sea. Miss Earhart was declared legally dead in 1939. There was speculation that she and Noonan were captured by the Japanese and executed on Saipan, but postwar investigations did not uncover evidence to support this theory.

ELY, Joseph (1881–1956). This Democratic governor of Massachusetts bitterly opposed the New Deal policies of **Franklin D. Roosevelt** (*see*) and supported Republican candidates for President in 1936 and 1944. Ely graduated from Williams College in 1903 and received a law degree from Harvard three years later. Entering politics in 1915, he was appointed a county district attorney. In 1930, Ely ran for governor on a platform urging the repeal of prohibition. His victory was attributed to Republican as well as Democratic support. Ely was reelected in 1932, and at the Democratic National Convention that year, he initially backed his friend Alfred E. Smith (1873–1944) for President. Four years later, Ely, who had resumed his law practice, joined a group that called themselves Jeffersonian Democrats. They crossed party lines to support the Republican nominee for President, **Alfred M. Landon** (*see*). Ely accused New Dealers of acting in contempt of the Supreme Court and warned that a "pink fringe" of Socialists and Communists had infiltrated the Presidency. In 1944, he announced his own candidacy for President in an effort to draw Democratic support away from Roosevelt and prevent his nomi-

Empire State Building

nation. When Roosevelt was nominated for a fourth term, Ely threw his support to Republican Thomas E. Dewey (1902–1971), who lost.

EMPIRE STATE BUILDING. Rising 102 stories (1,250 feet), the Empire State Building in New York City was for forty years the world's tallest building. It was erected in 1930–1931 on the site (Fifth Avenue, between 33rd and 34th Streets) of the old Waldorf-Astoria Hotel by a group headed by New York financier John J. Raskob (1879–1950). The firm of Shreve, Lamb, and Harmon was awarded the gold medal of the Architectural League in 1931 for its designs for the mammoth commercial building, which houses about 25,000 tenants. It boasts 65 automated passenger elevators and attracts more than 1,500,000 visitors annually to its observation terraces on the 86th and 102nd floors. The top of the structure—which was increased in height by 222 feet with the addition of a television tower in 1951 —is visible from all five boroughs of New York City. On July 28, 1945, a B-25 bomber, flying in fog, crashed into the north side of the building, killing the two crew members and several persons working on the 79th floor and hurling one engine completely through the building. The Empire State Building has since been topped by three others in the U.S. and Canada. The tallest building in the world is now the CNR Tower, Toronto, Ontario, which rises to a height of 1,821 feet.

F

FARLEY, James Aloysius (born 1888). A powerful New York politician who was chairman of the Democratic National Committee from 1932 to 1940, "Big Jim" Farley was instrumental in securing the Presidential nomination for **Franklin D. Roosevelt** (*see*) in 1932. Farley also managed the ensuing campaign that put Roosevelt in the White House. He then served as Postmaster General of the United States from 1933 to 1940. Born in Grassy Point, New York, Farley graduated from Packard Commercial School in New York City in 1906 before entering business as a bookkeeper. By 1926, he owned his own building firm, and three years later he became president (1929–1933) of the General Building Supply Company. Always interested in politics, Farley held a number of local and county offices in New York State before serving a year (1923–1924) in the New York Assembly and then becoming chairman of the New York State Athletic Commission (1925–1933). As the chairman (1930–1944) of the New York State Democratic Committee, Farley employed his impressive political connections and expertise on behalf of Roosevelt's candidacy for governor of New York in 1928 and his bid for the Presidency four years later. Rewarded with the office of Postmaster General, Farley again skillfully managed the victorious Roosevelt campaign in 1936. However, he broke with the President four years later, when Roosevelt declared his intention to seek a third term. After a vain effort to capture the Democratic nomination for himself, Farley resigned from the cabinet and the Democratic National Committee in 1940 and returned to business. In 1941, he became director and chairman of the board of the Coca-Cola Export Corporation. In 1958, Farley sought the New York Democratic nomination for the Senate, but his bid was unsuccessful. Farley has described his life and political experiences in *Behind the Ballots* (1938) and *Jim Farley's Story, the Roosevelt Years* (1948).

FARRELL, James Thomas (1904–1979). A novelist in the naturalist tradition of Theodore Dreiser (1871–1945), Farrell is best remembered for his trilogy *Studs Lonigan.* Born and raised in Chicago, Farrell made that city the

James T. Farrell

setting of many of his novels. He also used his own experiences as a pupil in Roman Catholic schools and later at the University of Chicago as a basis for many of his plots. After working as a clerk, salesman, and newspaper reporter, Farrell began writing a series of novels describing the life of a working-class, Irish-American youth who was a product of Chicago's squalid South Side. The first book, *Young Lonigan: A Boyhood in Chicago,* was published in 1932. It was followed two years later by *The Young Manhood of Studs Lonigan,* in which Farrell described Studs' moral downfall as he became involved in criminal activities. The third book, *Judgment Day,* published in 1935, portrayed his final defeat and death. Considered Farrell's masterpiece, the trilogy has remained a classic social documentary. The author wrote another cycle of novels between 1936 and 1953 about Danny O'Neill, a character similar to Studs Lonigan. In 1963, Farrell published the first of a projected series of four books about a University of Chicago student during the 1920s who abandoned his Catholicism and searched to discover his own identity. Farrell's other writings

include several collections of short stories and his *Collected Poems* (1965).

FIRST SCOTTSBORO CASE. *See* **Scottsboro Boys.**

G

GARNER, John Nance (1868–1967). Plain-spoken "Cactus Jack" Garner served nearly half his 98 years in public office, including two terms (1933–1941) as Vice-President of the United States under President **Franklin D. Roosevelt** (*see*). Born in a log cabin in Texas, Garner was educated in country schools and was admitted to the bar in 1890. While serving in the Texas legislature (1898–1902), he created a legislative district for himself and was elected to the House of Representatives in 1902. Garner served in the House for 30 years, becoming Speaker in 1931. A movement for his nomination as the Democratic Presidential candidate was begun in 1932. Garner entered the California primary and defeated both Roosevelt and Alfred E. Smith (1873–1944). However, he was unable to achieve the nomination after three ballots at the party's national convention and threw his support to Roosevelt on the next ballot. Garner reluctantly agreed to run for Vice-President to balance the ticket geographically. In the early days of the New Deal, he worked well with Roosevelt, but he became alarmed as the President sought increased executive powers. He particularly objected to Roosevelt's court-packing scheme (*see pp. 1252–1258*). Garner was certain that 1940 was his year to run for President, but when Roosevelt decided to run for a third term, he retired to Texas. Garner later referred to the office of Vice-President as an "unnecessary office," and in 1960, when Lyndon B. Johnson (1908–1973)

was offered the Democratic Vice-Presidential nomination, he told him that the office was "not worth a pitcher of warm spit" because "the Vice-President is just a waiting boy, waiting in case something happens to the President."

GATTY, Harold. *See* **Post, Wiley.**

GEORGE, Walter Franklin (1878–1957). George was a conservative Senator (1922–1957) from Georgia who first gained national prominence in 1938 when President **Franklin D. Roosevelt** (*see*) tried unsuccessfully to prevent his reelection to the Senate. Although a Democrat, George had opposed some of Roosevelt's New Deal measures and his attempt to reorganize the Supreme Court in 1937 (*see pp. 1252–1258*). George, a successful lawyer who never lost an election, was elected to his first political office, that of solicitor of the Vienna, Georgia, city court, in 1907. He subsequently held various judicial positions, the most important of which was as associate justice of the Georgia supreme court (1917–1922). Upon being elected to the Senate in 1922, George exerted a strong influence on foreign-policy and tax legislation, especially while serving as chairman of the Foreign Relations Committee (1940–1941 and 1955–1957) and of the Senate Finance Committee (1941–1947 and 1949–1952). An exponent of neutrality before World War II, George reversed his position after the outbreak of the war in Europe. He fought for the passage of the Lend-Lease Act in 1941, which authorized aid to Britain and other nations whose defense Roosevelt considered vital, and in 1945 he urged the ratification of the United Nations Charter. In March, 1955, George proposed that a Big Four "summit" meeting of the heads of the United States, Britain, France, and the Soviet Union be held as soon as possible. This led to the Geneva Conference the following July. At the time of his death, George was America's special ambassador to NATO, a position to which President Dwight D. Eisenhower (1890–1969) appointed him in 1956, when George announced that he would not seek reelection.

GERSHWIN, George (1898–1937). Gershwin was a leading American composer who is best remembered for his orchestral piece *Rhapsody in Blue* and the great number of songs he wrote for the musical stage. The Brooklyn-born musician took classical piano lessons as a child but was attracted to jazz at an early age. He left high school at 15 to work as a piano player in a music publishing house. Three years later, he published his first popular song, *When You Want 'Em, You Can't Get 'Em*. In 1919, Gershwin composed the entire score for the musical comedy *La, La, Lucille*. At the same time, his first hit song, *Swanee,* was recorded by Al Jolson (1888–1950). From 1920 to 1924, Gershwin composed the

CULVER PICTURES

George Gershwin

scores for the annual revues of *George White's Scandals.* He was the first to treat jazz as serious music in a one-act opera, *Blue Monday* (1922). The opera was performed as part of the *Scandals* in 1923, but it was unpopular. However, conductor Paul Whiteman (1891–1967) was impressed with the work and requested Gershwin to compose a jazz symphony. Gershwin accordingly wrote *Rhapsody in Blue* for piano and orchestra. The piece was first played in 1924 in a concert at Aeolian Hall in New York City. The rhythmic vitality and spirited melodies of the *Rhapsody* have made it the most frequently performed orchestral work written by an American. The next year, Gershwin was commissioned by the New York Symphony Society to compose a piece, which resulted in the *Concerto in F.* It was followed by *Three Piano Preludes* (1926), *An American in Paris* (1928), *Second Rhapsody* (1932), and *Cuban Overture* (1932). Gershwin's most ambitious work was *Porgy and Bess* (1935), a folk opera written for an all-black cast. With his brother Ira (1896–1983) writing most of the lyrics, Gershwin also composed scores for many Broadway plays and Hollywood films. His more popular musicals included *Lady, Be Good!* (1924), *Oh, Kay!* (1926), *Girl Crazy* (1930), and *Of Thee I Sing* (1931), the first musical comedy to be awarded the Pulitzer Prize for drama (1932). Gershwin died in Hollywood of a brain tumor at the age of 39.

GLASS, Carter (1858–1946). A Democrat from Virginia, Glass served as Secretary of the Treasury (1918–1920) and was a member of both houses of Congress. At the age of 14, Glass was apprenticed to a printer, and he subsequently became a reporter, city editor, editor, and owner of two Lynchburg, Virginia, newspapers,

the *Daily News* and the *Daily Advance.* While a state senator (1899–1903), he was elected to fill a vacancy in the House of Representatives and was reelected nine times, serving there until 1918. As chairman of the House Committee on Banking and Currency, Glass was instrumental in getting Congress in 1913 to enact the Federal Reserve Bank Act, which established the Federal Reserve System. Five years later, he was appointed Secretary of the Treasury by President Woodrow Wilson (1856–1924). In 1920, Glass left the cabinet in order to serve out the unexpired term of Virginia Senator Thomas S. Martin (1847–1919), who had died. Glass subsequently served in the Senate until his own death. He turned down an offer by President **Franklin D. Roosevelt** (*see*) in 1933 to resume the post of Treasury Secretary. Although Glass supported Roosevelt's foreign policy, he was so opposed to the President's monetary and New Deal policies that Roosevelt nicknamed him the Unreconstructed Rebel.

GOOD-NEIGHBOR POLICY. *See* **Roosevelt, Franklin D.**

GREAT DEPRESSION. *See* **Black Tuesday.**

H

HAUPTMANN, Bruno Richard. *See* **Lindbergh, Charles A.**

HOPPER, Edward (1882–1967). Hopper was a famous American painter and etcher whose most characteristic works are realistic, clear-cut, and light-filled representations of urban scenes or landscapes. His paintings usually omit human figures and frequently convey a feeling of intense loneliness (*see p. 1234*). A native of upstate New York, Hopper studied in New York City under Robert

Henri (1865–1929) and other artists from 1900 to 1906. During the next four years, he made three trips to Europe, spending most of his time in Paris but also visiting Belgium, England, Germany,

Edward Hopper

Holland, and Spain. A dedicated realist, Hopper was not particularly influenced by contemporary art trends. During the early years of his career, he supported himself by working as an illustrator and commercial artist. About 1915, he stopped painting in oil and subsequently won substantial recognition as an etcher before returning to oil painting in 1924. After the mid-1920s, Hopper began to enjoy considerable success as both an oil painter and watercolorist and was able to give up working as a commercial artist to earn his living. In 1933, the Museum of Modern Art in New York City gave him a retrospective exhibition, which firmly established his reputation as one of the leading painters in the American realist tradition. Hopper summed up his artistic credo in saying, "My aim in painting has always been the most exact transcription possible of my most intimate impressions of nature."

I

ICKES, Harold Le Claire (1874–1952). As Secretary of the Interior (1933–1946) under Presidents **Franklin D. Roosevelt** (*see*) and Harry S Truman (1884–1972), Ickes was one of the most powerful—and controversial—figures in high government office. During the Depression, he was in charge of implementing many of the New Deal recovery measures, while serving as head (1933–1939) of the Public Works Administration (PWA). Later, he controlled the coal and petroleum industries with a firm hand during World War II. A native of Pennsylvania, Ickes graduated from the University of Chicago in 1897. He worked for three years as a newspaper reporter and later returned to the University of Chicago for a law degree (1907). He subsequently set up a law practice in Chicago. Ickes had been immersed in politics as a relentless crusader for reform since 1897. Although a Republican, he renounced party orthodoxy to support the Progressive (Bull Moose) Party of former President Theodore Roosevelt (1858–1919) in 1912 and backed liberal Republicans for many years thereafter. In 1932, he endorsed the Democratic ticket, and F. D. R. named him to his cabinet after the election. A man of ability, energy, and integrity, "Honest Harold"—as his numerous enemies sarcastically called him—demanded the same qualities from his colleagues and stated his opinions bluntly. He once accused **Huey Long** (*see*) of Louisiana of "halitosis of the intellect." In 1944, when Republican Thomas E. Dewey (1902–1971) announced his candidacy for the Presidency, Ickes observed that Dewey reminded him of the little man on the wedding cake. While heading the Interior Department, Ickes, a long-time champion of civil rights,

did much to improve the status of American Indians and protect their lands and culture. Although he drew criticism for his time-consuming review of all programs he administered as chief of the PWA, Ickes directed the huge agency with scrupulous honesty. His efforts were influential in reducing public-utilities rates and creating low-cost housing. As a special fuels administrator during the war, Ickes exercised virtually dictatorial powers in coordinating fuel industries for the wartime needs of the nation. Ickes was retained as Secretary of the Interior when Truman assumed the Presidency in 1945, but he resigned the following year after a dispute over a Truman appointee, whom Ickes charged with conflict of interest. He then devoted himself to writing and practicing law. A sharp critic of the press, Ickes charged that American newspapers were often subservient to business interests in their handling of the news. His book, *The New Democracy* (1934), is an explanation of the New Deal philosophy. His three-volume *Secret Diary of Harold L. Ickes* (1953–1954), an account of the early period of the New Deal, appeared after his death.

J

JOHNSON, Hugh Samuel (1882–1942). This former army officer served as head of the National Recovery Administration (NRA), which was created in 1933 as an emergency measure to help the nation's faltering economy during the Depression. Born in Fort Scott, Kansas, Johnson graduated from West Point in 1903. In 1916, he accompanied General John J. Pershing (1860–1948) on a punitive expedition to Mexico. During World War I, Johnson served on the War Industries Board and helped write the Selective Service

Act, which was passed by Congress in 1917. He subsequently administered the draft. Johnson resigned from the army in 1919 and entered private business. Fourteen years later, President **Franklin D. Roosevelt** (*see*) organized the NRA, placing Johnson in charge and creating four boards to assist him. For a year, Johnson supervised the drawing up and enforcement of industry-wide codes for fair business practices to "eliminate eye-gouging and knee-groining and ear-chewing" in commerce. Although thousands of businessmen pledged their support, leading manufacturers took advantage of the voluntary agreements at the expense of labor unions. Temperamental and impetuous, Johnson was soon denouncing "chiselers." His violent language did much to destroy any existing rapport between the government and industry. Finally, in 1934, Roosevelt asked him to resign. Johnson worked for the rest of his life as a columnist and radio commentator, except for a brief time in 1935 when he was director of the Works Progress Administration (WPA) for New York City.

JONES, Robert ("Bobby"), Jr. (1902–1971). Bobby Jones is the only player in golf history to have won the United States Open, the National Amateur, the British Open, and the British Amateur Tournaments in the same year. The Georgia-born golfer won his first tournament at the age of nine. Five years later, he won the Georgia amateur championship. In 1917, Jones became the Southern amateur champion. While perfecting his game, he found time to attend the Georgia School of Technology, Harvard, and Emory University Law School. Admitted to the bar in 1928, he established a law practice in Atlanta. In 1923, Jones won his first major tournament, the United States Open. He was first in this tournament four

times (1923, 1926, 1929, and 1930), the British Open three times (1926, 1927, and 1930), and the National Amateur five times (1924, 1925, 1927, 1928, and 1930). In 1930, he achieved the so-called grand slam, winning these three tournaments in addition to the British Amateur (*see p. 1212*). Afterward, Jones retired from competition to devote himself to his law practice. In 1949, a crippling ailment forced him to give up golf altogether. However, he remained active in golfing circles, serving as president of the Augusta National Golf Club, where the Masters Tournament is held annually. He has designed or remodeled more than 200 golf courses in this nation and abroad.

K

KELLOGG, Frank Billings (1856–1937). As Secretary of State under Calvin Coolidge (1872–1933), Kellogg promoted the signing of the Kellogg-Briand Pact, a treaty designed to outlaw war that was ultimately signed by 62 nations. For his efforts, he was awarded the Nobel Peace Prize in 1929. Kellogg was born in upstate New York but was raised in Minnesota, where his family moved when he was nine. With no formal education beyond grade school, he clerked in a law office and was admitted to the bar in 1877. Kellogg specialized in corporate law. As a special government counsel appointed by President Theodore Roosevelt (1858–1919), he gained a reputation as a "trustbuster." His most famous case was the prosecution of the Standard Oil Company from 1910 to 1911. Elected to the Senate in 1916, Kellogg served one term and was defeated for reelection in 1922. He returned to his law practice until 1924, when Coolidge appointed him ambassador to Great Britain. Kellogg returned to Washington,

D.C., the following year to become Secretary of State. His best-known accomplishment as Secretary was the negotiation with Aristide Briand (1862–1932), the French foreign minister, of the antiwar pact that bore their names. Kellogg expanded the concept of the pact by negotiating arbitration treaties with 61 other nations. He also promoted the Geneva Naval Conference in 1927, an effort to limit naval armaments. However, both it and the Kellogg-Briand Pact proved unenforceable in the 1930s. Kellogg later served as a judge (1930–1935) on the World Court at The Hague.

KENNEDY, Joseph Patrick (1888–1969). A controversial self-made millionaire and diplomat, Kennedy was the father of President John F. Kennedy (1917–1963), Senator Robert F. Kennedy (1925–1968), and Senator Edward M. Kennedy (born 1932). "Joe" Kennedy was the son of a first-generation Irish immigrant who became the owner of a string of saloons and was an important Democratic ward boss in Boston. Taught from early youth the importance of money and power, Kennedy decided to enroll at Harvard, then a bold move for an Irish Catholic. Upon graduation in 1912, he became a bank examiner in order to learn the business. Two years later, Kennedy borrowed heavily to save his father's failing bank and was elected president of the Columbia Trust Company. As the youngest bank president in America, Kennedy was an acceptable suitor for Rose Fitzgerald (born 1891), the daughter of Boston's ex-mayor and most important politician, John F. "Honey Fitz" Fitzgerald (1863–1950). They were married in October, 1914, and had nine children. Kennedy's devotion to his wife and children led to a strong sense of family solidarity, which helped the Kennedys through the tragedies that seemed to plague them—Joseph, Jr. (1915–1944), his father's favorite, was killed flying a mission during World War II; Rosemary (born 1919) was eventually confined to an institution for the mentally retarded; Kathleen (1920–1948) was killed in a private-airplane crash; and John and Robert were victims of assassins' bullets. During World War I, Kennedy was the assistant general manager of the Fore River shipyard of the Bethlehem Steel Company and had his first dealings with **Franklin D. Roosevelt** (*see*), then Assistant Secretary of the Navy. When the war ended, Kennedy entered the investment business. By 1929, he had made his mark in securities, real estate, and the new movie industry. Kennedy foresaw the stock-market crash and withdrew most of his money early in 1929. At the 1932 Democratic National Convention, he was one of the few business tycoons supporting Roosevelt's candidacy for President. After Roosevelt's election, Kennedy anticipated the end of prohibition and went to England, where he obtained exclusive rights to import certain brands of Scotch and gin. In 1934, Roosevelt appointed Kennedy the first chairman of the Securities and Exchange Commission. He served just over a year, long enough to firmly establish the SEC as an effective government regulatory agency. During the 1936 campaign, Kennedy wrote a book, *I'm For Roosevelt,* and was subsequently appointed chairman of the Maritime Commission. As ambassador to Great Britain in 1937, Kennedy supported the appeasement policy toward Germany of Prime Minister Neville Chamberlain (1869–1940). After England entered World War II, Kennedy did not favor American aid to the Allies and thought England's defeat inevitable—views for which he was roundly criticized. Kennedy returned to America in 1940 and halfheartedly supported Roosevelt's bid for a third term that year but resigned his post after Roosevelt's reelection. After the Japanese attack on Pearl Harbor in 1941, Kennedy volunteered his services to the President. His offer was not accepted, and the only federal post Kennedy ever held again was on a 1949 government reorganization commission. He turned his attention to real estate and bought a great deal of property in Manhattan that he later sold at huge profits. His most famous real-estate venture was the purchase of the Merchandise Mart in Chicago for $13,000,000 in 1945. Its value soared to $75,000,000 by the mid-1960s, and Kennedy received his initial investment every year in rent. Kennedy sought to avoid the limelight when his son John entered politics. In December, 1961, he suffered a paralytic stroke from which he never fully recovered.

KNOX, Wilson Franklin ("Frank") (1874–1944). A prominent Republican newspaper publisher, Frank Knox was appointed Secretary of the Navy in 1940 by President **Franklin D. Roosevelt** (*see*) in a move designed to give his cabinet a bipartisan structure and to bolster national unity in a time of crisis. Born in Boston, Knox had served with Theodore Roosevelt (1858–1919) in the Rough Riders during the Spanish-American War in 1898. He later worked in Michigan, first as a newspaper reporter (1894–1901) in Grand Rapids, then as the publisher (1901–1912) of the Sault Sainte Marie *News*. In 1912, after working on Theodore Roosevelt's unsuccessful Progressive Party campaign, he moved to New Hampshire, where he bought the Manchester *Leader*. He merged it with the Manchester *Union* the following year, remaining its publisher until his death. After over-

Frank Knox

seas service in France during World War I, Knox became a colonel in the Field Artillery Reserve. In 1927, he joined the vast newspaper enterprise of William Randolph Hearst (1863–1951), becoming general manager of all Hearst newspapers the following year. Knox resigned from the Hearst press in 1931 to become publisher of the Chicago *Daily News,* which he controlled until his death. Knox's vigorously anti-New Deal editorials led to his nomination as the Vice-Presidential candidate on the unsuccessful Republican ticket in 1936. When America's entry into World War II seemed imminent, Knox, then Roosevelt's Navy Secretary (1940–1944), stressed the need for American naval supremacy. After the Japanese attack on Pearl Harbor on December 7, 1941, he was charged with the task of building a strong American navy in both the Pacific and Atlantic Oceans, and he helped make the United States fleet the most powerful naval force in the world. He died in office after United States forces had taken the offensive on both fronts.

L

LA GUARDIA, Fiorello Henry (1882–1947). The popular and colorful mayor of New York City for three terms (1934–1945), the "Little Flower" (as his first name was translated from Italian) promoted slum clearance, public housing, parks and playgrounds, bridges and airports, and numerous other public improvements. He fought organized crime and municipal graft and was himself a model of incorruptible honesty. La Guardia was born in New York. His mother was Jewish. His father, an Italian immigrant, was an army bandmaster, and Fiorello grew up on military bases, chiefly in Arizona. After the death of his father in 1898, La Guardia moved with his family to Europe, where he was employed at American consulates in Hungary and Austria. Returning to the United States in 1906, he worked as an interpreter (he spoke at least six languages) for the Immigration Service at Ellis Island while studying law at night and was admitted to the bar in 1910. Short, rotund, and outspoken, La Guardia was elected to the House of Representatives on the Republican ticket in 1916. However, he resigned the following year to serve in World War I on the Italian-Austrian front, where he was decorated and commissioned a major for his services as a pilot, flight instructor, and propagandist. La Guardia presided over the New York City board of aldermen from 1920 to 1921 and then was reelected to the House in 1923. Over the next 10 years, he distinguished himself as one of Congress' leading progressive legislators, championing labor reforms and women's suffrage and opposing child labor, prohibition, racism, censorship, and imperialism. He was co-sponsor of the Norris-La Guardia Anti-Injunction Act of 1932, which curbed strikebreaking by judicial injunction and banned "yellow dog" (antiunion) contracts. In 1929, La Guardia was defeated for mayor of New York by the incumbent, James J. "Jimmy" Walker (1881–1946). However, running as a Fusion Party candidate four years later, La Guardia was swept into office by a coalition of supporters drawn from all political parties. Combining superb administrative abilities with political craft and a showman's flair (*see p. 1246*), La Guardia restored integrity to the city administration after the corruption of the Walker regime —while also finding time to read comic strips over the radio during a newspaper strike. During World War II, La Guardia, a friend of President **Franklin D. Roosevelt** (*see*), briefly directed (1941–1942) the Office of Civilian Defense. In 1946, the year after his retirement as mayor, he headed the United Nations Relief and Rehabilitation Administration (UNRRA). The Pulitzer Prize-winning musical *Fiorello!*, which opened on Broadway in 1959, was based on his life.

LANDON, Alfred Mossman (1887–1987). As the Republican Presidential candidate in 1936, "Alf" Landon suffered an overwhelming defeat at the hands of **Franklin D. Roosevelt** (*see*). Born in Pennsylvania, Landon moved to Kansas and received a law degree from the University of Kansas in 1908. After four years as a banker, he switched to drilling oil and became an independent producer. Landon supported Progressive Theodore Roosevelt (1858–1919) in 1912. He was appointed private secretary to the governor of Kansas in 1922 and was subsequently recognized as the leader of the state's liberal Republicans. In 1928, Landon became the chairman of the Republican Central Committee in Kansas. He was elected governor in 1932, and in two terms compiled a creditable

Alfred M. Landon

record, by reducing taxes and balancing the state budget. Landon was nominated for President at the Republican National Convention in 1936 on the first ballot. Conservative **Frank Knox** (*see*) was named his running mate. During the campaign, Landon modified his liberal views and received the support of many conservatives. However, Roosevelt's majority exceeded 11,000,000 votes, and Landon received just eight electoral votes—from Maine and Vermont. Landon never again sought political office. He has devoted his time to the management of his oil business and his three radio stations in Kansas. In 1962, Landon told an interviewer, "I'm an oilman who never made his million. A lawyer who never had a case. And a politician who only carried Maine and Vermont."

LAWRENCE, Ernest Orlando (1901–1958). A noted scientist, Lawrence invented the cyclotron, or atom smasher, which opened the new field of nuclear physics. Born in South Dakota, Lawrence received his Ph.D. from Yale in

1925, and three years later, was named an associate professor of physics at the University of California at Berkeley. Lawrence conceived the cyclotron in 1931 and founded the Radiation Laboratory at the University of California to house it. Eight years later, he received the Nobel Prize in physics for his research in atomic structure and transmutation. After the Japanese attack on Pearl Harbor in December, 1941, Lawrence, Harold C. Urey (1893–1981), and Arthur H. Compton (1892–1962) were named program chiefs of the Manhattan Project, which was set up to develop the atom bomb. After World War II, Lawrence and his associates produced artificially radioactive elements in the cyclotron that proved useful in nuclear, chemical, and biological research. One year before his death, he received the $50,000 Fermi Award from the Atomic Energy Commission.

Ernest O. Lawrence

CULVER PICTURES

LEWIS, John Llewellyn (1880–1969). A powerful independent labor leader with a flair for the dramatic, Lewis was president of the United Mine Workers (U.M.W.) for 40 years (*see p. 1223*). The son of a Welsh coal miner, Lewis was born in Iowa and went to work in the coal mines himself at the age of 17. In 1906, the young miner was elected a delegate to the U. M. W. convention. He was a talented organizer and speaker. By 1920, he was president of the U. M. W. Favoring industrial rather than craft unions, Lewis in 1935 organized the Committee for Industrial Organization (later the Congress of Industrial Organizations, or C. I. O.) and served as its president. The American Federation of Labor (A. F. L.) expelled the unions affiliated with the C. I. O. in November, 1936, but the C. I. O. continued to grow under Lewis' leadership, and numerous unions seceded on their own from the A. F. L. to join the C. I. O. Almost immediately Lewis launched a series of successful strikes in which miners employed the new technique of the sit-down. Lewis had originally supported **Franklin D. Roosevelt** (*see*) and his New Deal, but in 1940 he backed Republican Wendell L. Willkie (1892–1944). He resigned as president of the C. I. O. when Willkie lost. Two years later, Lewis led the U. M. W. out of the C. I. O. because of differences with the new president, Philip Murray (1886–1952). During World War II, Lewis was condemned by the War Labor Board because of the many strikes called by the U. M. W. When Lewis staged a 59-day soft-coal strike in the spring of 1946, the federal government finally stepped in and seized control of the mines. He called another strike that November, in defiance of a federal court order, and was fined $10,000. The union was fined $3,500,000. That same year, however, Lewis persuaded the coal industry to finance a pension fund for his workers, the first such fund obtained by organized labor in America. In addition, the U. M. W. was readmitted to the A. F. L., and Lewis was made a vice-president. In December, 1947, although he was a known foe of communism, Lewis refused to sign the loyalty oath required of union officers by the Taft-Hartley Act, and he again took the U. M. W. out of the A. F. L. In the 1950s, Lewis and his union became less aggressive. When the A. F. L. and the C. I. O. merged in 1955, the U. M. W. did not join. Lewis retired as president of the union in 1960 but remained influential in U. M. W. affairs until his death in 1969.

LIBERTY LEAGUE. Among the most determined and well-financed organizations that attacked the New Deal policies of President **Franklin D. Roosevelt** (*see*) was the Liberty League. Organized in 1934 to combat the alleged "inroads of socialism" into the federal government after Roosevelt took office in 1933, the league was an undisguised "rich man's lobby." As such, it bitterly opposed the President's policy of redistributing national resources by imposing high taxes on the incomes of corporations and the wealthy. Among the best known political backers of the league were Massachusetts Governor **Joseph B. Ely** (*see*) and two former Democratic Presidential candidates, John W. Davis (1873–1955), the standard-bearer in 1924, and Alfred E. Smith (1873–1944), the party nominee in 1928. Financier John J. Raskob (1879–1950) and members of the industrially powerful du Pont family were prominent among the many conservative millionaire supporters of the league. Roosevelt, who had steadily moved away from courting businessmen to concentrate on enlisting the support of labor, minority groups, and the poor, denounced his enemies as selfish "economic royalists." "They are unanimous in their *hate* for *me,*" he said, *"and I welcome their hatred."* The Liberty League was unsuccessful and short-lived, fading from the national scene after its futile support of Republican candidate **Alfred M. Landon** (*see*) in the 1936 Presidential election. After his reelection, Roosevelt scoffed at the league for having ascribed to him "the worst features of Ivan the Terrible, Machiavelli, Judas Iscariot, Henry VIII, Charlotte Corday, and Jesse James."

LINDBERGH, Charles Augustus, Jr. (1902–1974). Lindbergh became world famous as the "Lone Eagle" who made the first solo nonstop flight between New York and Paris in 1927. After the tragic kidnapping and murder of his infant son in 1932, he retired from the limelight. Before the United States' entry into World War II, he received widespread publicity as an isolationist. In recent years, he has actively promoted conservation around the world. Lind-

Lindbergh suits up for his historic flight across the Atlantic in 1927.

bergh, whose father, Charles A. Lindbergh, Sr. (1859–1924), was a prominent United States Representative, was born in Detroit. After attending the University of Wisconsin (1920–1922), he studied aviation. While working as an airmail service pilot on the Chicago-St. Louis route in 1926, Lindbergh decided to try for the $25,000 prize offered by the New York hotel owner Raymond B. Orteig (1870–1939) for the first nonstop flight between New York and Paris. Backed by a group of St. Louis businessmen, Lindbergh ordered a single-engine monoplane, which he named *Spirit of St. Louis.* He then supervised its construction at the Ryan Airlines factory in San Diego, California. Lindbergh flew the craft from San Diego to Curtiss Field, Long Island—with a stopover in St. Louis —in a record 21 hours and 20 minutes (May 10–12, 1927). Then, on the foggy, rainy morning of May 20, 1927, Lindbergh left Roosevelt Field, Long Island, for France. When he touched down at Le Bourget Airfield, near Paris, 33 and a half hours later, he was wildly acclaimed throughout the world. He was promoted from captain to colonel in the Air Corps Reserve and received many honors, including the Medal of Honor. He subsequently made goodwill flights in America, Mexico, Central America, and the Caribbean. In 1929, Lindbergh married Anne Spencer Morrow (born 1906). On March 1, 1932, their infant son, Charles Augustus III, was kidnapped from their home in Hopewell, New Jersey. The couple paid $50,000 in ransom, but on the following May 12, the child's battered body was found near Hopewell. The crime shocked the nation and resulted in the passage of the so-called Lindbergh laws. Among other things, these laws made interstate kidnapping a federal offense punishable by death. In September,

1934, Bruno Richard Hauptmann (1899–1936), a German-born carpenter, was found with part of the ransom. In the sensational murder trial that followed, he was convicted and eventually electrocuted in April, 1936. Seeking seclusion, the Lindberghs moved to Europe in December, 1935. In 1938, Lindbergh made surveys of the air power of France, Britain, the Soviet Union, and Germany. He returned to the United States the following year, convinced of German air superiority. A vigorous advocate of American neutrality, he became a leader of the America First Committee which resulted in his being considered a Nazi sympathizer by many people. Lindbergh subsequently resigned his commission in the Air Corps Reserve in April, 1941. After America entered the war that December, Lindbergh volunteered for active service but was turned down because he would not recant his earlier antiwar statements. Despite government opposition, he worked as a civilian consultant to the Ford Motor Company and the United Aircraft Corporation. In 1944, when he went to the Pacific as a civilian technician, Lindbergh flew about 50 combat missions and was unofficially credited with having shot down at least one Japanese aircraft. After the war, the Lindberghs settled in Connecticut. He subsequently became a consultant to the United States Air Force and to Pan American World Airways, of which he is also a director. In 1954, Lindbergh was recommissioned a brigadier general in the Air Force Reserve. His writings include *Of Flight and Life* (1948) and *The Spirit of St. Louis* (1953), the 1954 winner of the Pulitzer Prize for autobiography. Mrs. Lindbergh has written several books, including *North to the Orient* (1935) and *Listen! the Wind* (1938), which are both about her flying experiences with her husband; *Gift From the Sea* (1955), a volume of prose and poetry; and *Dearly Beloved* (1962), a novel.

LONG, Huey Pierce (1893–1935). As governor and later a Senator, the colorful, controversial Long exercised dictatorial control over Louisiana, while at the same time improving social and economic conditions in his native state. He had a photographic memory and passed his bar examination in 1915 after completing just eight months of a three-year course at Tulane University. At the age of 24, Long was elected to the State Railroad Commission, which was renamed the Public Service Commission in 1921. As a commissioner (1918–1922) and later as chairman (1922–1926), he gained a statewide reputation by forcing the Standard Oil Company to pay higher taxes and by getting the local telephone and utility companies to lower their rates. Long ran for governor in 1924 and finished third. He succeeded in winning the governorship in 1928. As governor, Long rejected race baiting and addressed himself to the social and economic problems of his state. He constructed a network of free roads and bridges, eliminated the poll tax, and greatly increased expenditures for public education. His opponents saw him in a different light. They accused him of taking graft, using foul language, bribing legislators, and even seeking the assassination of a political foe. However, their attempt to impeach him in 1929 was defeated by Long and his powerful political machine. The governor called himself Kingfish and enjoyed leading the Louisiana State University band. Once, after L. S. U. had lost a football game by a score of seven to six, he tried to get the legislature to outlaw the point after touchdown. In 1930, Long was elected to the Senate, but he did not take his seat until January, 1932, after his hand-

picked candidate had won the Democratic nomination for governor. In the Senate, he broke with the administration of **Franklin D. Roosevelt** (*see*) and conducted filibusters against a number of New Deal measures. Long developed his own program to eliminate poverty, "Share Our Wealth," which included an annual minimum wage and free education from kindergarten through college. More than 27,000 Share Our Wealth clubs supported Long's program, and in August, 1935, he announced his intention to run for President the following year. In September, Long was in Baton Rouge to direct a special session of the legislature. On September 8, in the state capitol building, he was shot by Dr. Carl A. Weiss, the son-in-law of a political opponent. Weiss was killed immediately by Long's bodyguards. Long died two days later, and 150,000 people attended his funeral. A Pulitzer Prize-winning novel, *All The King's Men* (1946), by Robert Penn Warren (born 1905), is based on Long's career. Long's brother Earl (1895–1960) served three terms as governor, and his son Russell (born 1918) has served in the Senate since 1949.

M

McPHERSON, Aimee Semple (1890–1944). A woman of great magnetism, with a powerful voice and untiring energy, "Sister Aimee" was an evangelist who founded the Angelus Temple in Los Angeles, where her congregation numbered more than 30,000 in the 1920s. She also established nearly 400 "lighthouses" (subsidiary churches) and 178 missionary outposts throughout the world. She was born Aimee Elizabeth Kennedy on a farm in Ontario, Canada. At the age of 17, against the wishes of her domineering

Aimee Semple McPherson

CULVER PICTURES

mother, Minnie ("Ma") Kennedy, she married a traveling Pentecostal minister, Robert Semple, and went with him to Hong Kong to do missionary work. Semple became ill and died, leaving Aimee to return to the United States with her infant girl, Roberta. After much indecision and wandering, she married Harold McPherson, a grocery clerk, and gave birth to a second child, Rolf. However, the marriage failed after a year, and Aimee took to the "sawdust trail" as an itinerant revivalist. With her two children and mother, Aimee campaigned thousands of miles throughout the country, preaching in tents, halls, auditoriums, and on street corners. After visiting Canada, New Zealand, and Australia, she settled in southern California in 1921, where her reputation as a faith healer, her personal dynamism, and her showmanship—she held meetings in boxing arenas and scattered literature from an airplane—won an immense following. The mammoth Angelus Temple, complete with thundering organ, radio station, adjacent theological seminary, and "Miracle Room" (which was soon filled with abandoned wheelchairs and crutches), was opened on January 1, 1923. Sister Aimee preached the "Foursquare Gospel"—the literal truth of the Bible; conversion; healing the sick through religion; and the Second Coming of Jesus Christ to the earth. Her sermons emphasized hope and happiness, rejecting the gloomy doomsday-and-hellfire message of most contemporary evangelists. She enlivened her meetings with pageants, music, dramas, pictures, and flamboyant sermons. She baptized almost 40,000 persons during her 21 years as head of the Temple. In one of the most publicized events of the era, Sister Aimee disappeared from a beach at Venice, California, on May 18, 1926. An extensive search failed to find her, and she was believed drowned. She reappeared 32 days later in Agua Prieta, Mexico, asserting that she had been kidnapped and imprisoned. However, rumors persisted—and substantial evidence was obtained—that she had been secretly living with the Temple's radio announcer. When the Los Angeles district attorney's office charged her with conspiracy to obstruct justice, Aimee's followers raised $250,000 to fight the indictment. After several months of stormy hearings and sensational publicity, the charges were suddenly dropped. Sister Aimee then wrote her autobiography, *In the Service of the King,* and later toured Europe, but her popularity declined. She married again in the 1930s but was divorced shortly afterward. Her last years were marred by public arguments with her mother and numerous lawsuits filed by disgruntled parishioners. After her death from an overdose of sleeping pills, she was buried in the famed Forest Lawn Memorial Park, a cemetery for Hollywood celebrities.

McREYNOLDS, James Clark (1862–1946). During his 27 years on the Supreme Court, James C. McReynolds voted against more of the New Deal measures advocated by President **Franklin D. Roosevelt** (*see*) than any other Associate Justice. One of the so-called Nine Old Men, he was a principal target in the President's unsuccessful attempt to expand the membership of the Court (*see pp. 1252–1258*). Born in Kentucky, McReynolds graduated from Vanderbilt University in 1882 and from the University of Virginia Law School two years later. He subsequently practiced law in Nashville, Tennessee, and taught law (1900–1903) at Vanderbilt. As Assistant Attorney General (1903–1907) he was extremely active in prosecuting violators of the Sherman Antitrust Act. Later, while engaged in private law practice in New York City, he served as a special assistant to the Attorney General in several antitrust cases. McReynolds was Attorney General (1913–1914) during the administration of Woodrow Wilson (1856–1924) and initiated several important antitrust actions against large corporations, including the American Telephone and Telegraph Company. As an Associate Justice (1914–1941) of the Supreme Court, McReynolds was noted for his defense of states' rights and for his conviction that many New Deal acts were unconstitutional.

MARSH, Reginald (1898–1954). Marsh was a painter and illustrator whose pictures often satirized life in New York City. The artist was born in Paris, where his parents, both American painters, then resided. After the family's return to the United States, Marsh enrolled at Yale. Upon graduation (1920), Marsh began doing illustrations and cartoons for the New York *Daily News, Vanity Fair, Harper's Bazaar,* and *The New Yorker.* He later studied at the Art Students League under John Sloan (1871–1951) and Kenneth Hayes Miller (1876–1952). Marsh painted many scenes of Greenwich Village, Coney Island, and the Bowery. His style was exuberant, realistic, and colorful, and his treatment was often so satirical that he was sometimes called the Hogarth of New York (*see p. 1233*). Marsh worked in a variety of media, including watercolors, oils, egg tempera, and washes. He also became known for his book illustrations and murals. Among the latter are the murals in the Post Office Building in Washington, D.C., and the Custom House in New York City.

MELLON, Andrew William (1855–1937). A Pittsburgh banker and industrialist who was one of the wealthiest men in the world, Mellon served as Secretary of the Treasury under three Presidents—Warren G. Harding (1865–1923), Calvin Coolidge (1872–1933), and Herbert Hoover (1874–1964)—and was one of the dominant

CULVER PICTURES

Andrew W. Mellon

government figures of his day. Born in Pittsburgh, Mellon, the son of a banker, left the Western University of Pennsylvania (now the University of Pittsburgh) in 1872 before graduation and entered business. He soon assumed leadership of the family banking house, which he rapidly expanded and diversified. Between 1889 and 1902, he organized the Union Trust Company of Pittsburgh, the Union Savings Bank, and the Mellon National Bank. Quick to see the potential of growing industries, Mellon helped found the Aluminum Company of America (Alcoa) and the Gulf Oil Company. He also acquired substantial holdings in coal, steel, shipbuilding, insurance, bridgebuilding, locomotives, hydroelectric power, and public utilities. A behind-the-scenes financial genius, Mellon was little known to the public when he was named to head the Treasury Department in 1921. He succeeded in reducing the national debt from more than $24,000,-000,000 in 1920 to about $16,-000,000,000 by 1930. However, he was the center of intense controversy for urging tax policies that favored big business and the rich at the expense of lower-income groups and for his opposition to veterans' bonuses and farm subsidies. Mellon's program for the settlement of debts owed by foreign nations after World War I was unsuccessful, because he refused to help European countries return to prosperity by lowering tariffs on goods imported to the United States. He left the Treasury Department in 1932 to become ambassador to Great Britain. After a year of service, he returned to private business. In 1935, the Internal Revenue Service charged Mellon with tax evasion, but the suit was eventually settled in his favor. In 1937, the year of his death, Mellon gave funds for the building of the National Gallery of Art in Washing-

Novelist Margaret Mitchell, left, attended the movie premiere of Gone With the Wind *in 1939 with her husband, John Marsh. Seated next to him is Clark Gable.*

ton, D.C., and contributed his own art collection, valued at more than $35,000,000, to it.

MILLIS, Walter (1899–1968). A journalist and historian, Millis specialized in writing on military and political affairs. After graduating from Yale in 1920, the Georgia-born writer joined the staff of the Baltimore *News.* He left the paper three years later to become an editorial writer for the New York *Sun and Globe.* In 1924, Millis was hired by the New York *Herald Tribune* as an editorial and staff writer, a position he held for the next 30 years. In addition, he became an editor-at-large for *Saturday Review.* His first important book, *The Martial Spirit,* an account of the Spanish-American War, was published in 1931. Four years later, in *The Road to War: 1914–1917,* Millis analyzed the origins of World War I. His opposition to the United States' entry into the war aligned Millis with isolationists in America. However, by 1940, he had reversed his position and was urging American intervention in World War II. That same year, he explored the causes of the war in *Why Europe Fights.* This was followed in 1946 by *The*

Last Phase, a study of the Nazi defeat. In 1951, Millis edited the diaries of Secretary of Defense James Forrestal (1892–1949). Three years later, he left the *Herald Tribune* to join the staff of the Center for the Study of Democratic Institutions in Santa Barbara, California. One of his best-known works, *Arms and Men,* was published in 1956. Millis' last book was *The Abolition of War* (1963). He later wrote a number of articles opposing the war in Vietnam.

MITCHELL, Margaret (1900–1949). Miss Mitchell was the author of *Gone With the Wind,* a novel about the Civil War that became one of the most popular best sellers in history. The Georgia-born writer attended Washington Seminary in Atlanta (1914–1918). After spending a year at Smith College, she returned to Georgia and joined the staff of the Atlanta *Journal* in 1922. Miss Mitchell worked as a reporter and feature writer for the newspaper until 1926, when an ankle injury forced her to resign. Encouraged by her husband, John R. Marsh, to continue her writing, Miss Mitchell began an account of the Civil War and Reconstruction

Billy Mitchell flew this pursuit plane shortly after being made a general in 1920.

periods. Published 10 years later as *Gone With the Wind,* the book sold 50,000 copies in a single day, and sales in the first year totaled nearly 1,500,000 copies. The novel portrayed the problems of the Old South and in particular the struggles of a Georgia belle, Scarlett O'Hara, to preserve the family plantation, Tara. For her book, the only one she ever published, Miss Mitchell was awarded the Pulitzer Prize for fiction in 1937. Two years later, the novel was made into a film that set box-office records (*see p. 1224*). Considered a screen classic, the movie is periodically revived. Miss Mitchell died in 1949 from injuries received when she was struck by an automobile.

MITCHELL, William Lendrum ("Billy") (1879–1936). An army officer and aviator, Billy Mitchell was an early champion of military air power whose controversial views led to his court-martial before World War II. Mitchell was born in Nice, France, a son of Senator John L. Mitchell (1842–1904) of Wisconsin. At the outbreak of the Spanish-American War in 1898, Mitchell left his studies at Columbian University

(now George Washington University) to enlist as an army private. After serving in Cuba and the Philippines, he received a regular commission in the signal corps in 1901. Eight years later, he graduated from the Army Staff College, and in 1913 he became—at the age of 33—the youngest officer ever appointed to the general staff. Mitchell became interested in aviation after observing a demonstration of the army's first airplanes in 1908. He subsequently took flying lessons at his own expense and became a skilled pilot. During World War I, Mitchell helped organize the air service of the American Expeditionary Force. After April, 1918, he led its air operations, becoming the first American officer to fly over enemy lines. That same year, he commanded nearly 1,500 Allied planes in a mass attack during the St. Mihiel offensive. Mitchell returned from the war a much-decorated hero, convinced of the value of air superiority. In 1919, he was appointed assistant chief of the air service and the next year promoted to brigadier general. During the early 1920s, Mitchell fought for increased independence of the air service. He urged the

creation of either a separate department of the air force or a single defense department in which air, sea, and ground forces would be coordinated. To promote his views before conservative, budget-conscious officials of the War Department, Mitchell wrote a number of articles and books and often spoke on the subject. To prove the potential of aircraft in naval warfare, in 1921 he dramatically sank the modern German battleship *Ostfriesland,* a war prize, in 23 minutes with six specially made one-ton bombs. As early as 1923, he reported that American defenses at Pearl Harbor on the Hawaiian island of Oahu were inadequate. However, Mitchell was so sharp in his criticism of the War Department that in 1925 he was relieved as assistant chief of the air service and demoted to colonel. After the crash of the navy dirigible *Shenandoah* that same year, Mitchell publicly charged the War Department with "incompetency, criminal negligence, and almost treasonable administration of the national defense." As a result, he was court-martialed for insubordination in a trial during which government officials refused to argue the validity of his accusations. Found guilty, Mitchell was suspended from duty for five years. Mitchell resigned his commission in 1926, retiring to raise cattle on a Virginia ranch. His views were later vindicated by the massive air operations of World War II. In 1942, many years after his death, Congress restored him to the rank of major general, and in 1946 it voted him a special Medal of Honor. A final vindication came in 1947 with the unification of the military services under the Department of Defense, at which time the air force was officially separated from the army.

MOLEY, Raymond. *See* **Brain Trust.**

N

NEW DEAL. *See* **Roosevelt, Franklin D.**

NYE, Gerald Prentice (1892–1971). As a Republican Senator from North Dakota (1925–1945), Nye was an outspoken champion of isolationism and a leading member of the rightist America First Committee. Nye, who was born in Wisconsin, was a newspaper editor and publisher in both his native state, Iowa, and North Dakota from 1911 until he became a Senator. During most of his journalistic and political career, he was also a leader of the North Dakota Nonpartisan League, which was set up by agrarian interests to prevent the state's economy from being dominated by outside interests. In Congress, Nye played an important role in the 1927 Senate investigation of illegal leasing of naval oil reserves, a scandal that became known as the Teapot Dome. From 1934 to 1936, he served as chairman of the Senate Munitions Investigating Committee—also known as the Nye Committee—which claimed that American bankers and munitions makers had made enormous profits during World War I and had provoked America's entry into that conflict. The committee's sensational disclosures strengthened the isolationist spirit in the United States and prepared the way for the passage of a series of neutrality acts between 1935 and 1937. The first of these in 1935 put an embargo on the shipment of munitions to belligerents. The following year, a second act revised the first to prohibit the granting of loans to warring nations, and in 1937 a third neutrality act outlawed civilian travel on belligerent vessels. Nye maintained his isolationist stand after the outbreak of World War II and failed to win reelection in 1944. In 1960, he was appointed to the Federal Housing Administration as a special assistant for housing for the elderly.

P

PANAY INCIDENT. On December 12, 1937, the *Panay*, a United States Navy gunboat patrolling the Yangtze River in China, was attacked and sunk by Japanese navy planes. Two American sailors were killed, as was the captain of one of three nearby Standard Oil tankers that were sunk the same afternoon. The incident caused a storm of protest in the United States, and many persons later regarded the gunboat as the first casualty of World War II. Earlier, in the summer of 1937, Japanese troops had invaded southern China. By late fall, they were closing in on Nanking, the *Panay*'s home port. Nine American and European business-

The Panay *slowly sinks after being bombed and strafed by Japanese planes in 1937.*

men and correspondents had taken refuge on the *Panay*, anticipating a Japanese take-over in Nanking. The vessel had been built in 1927 and was one of six gunboats specifically designed for patrolling the Yangtze to protect the rights and property of American businessmen and missionaries in China. The boat, which was lightly armed, carried a crew of four officers, 49 enlisted men, and about 12 Chinese deckhands. As a neutral, she displayed two large American flags, which were spotlighted at night to ensure against a Japanese attack. In the afternoon of December 11, a Saturday, artillery shells, presumably directed at Nanking, landed near the *Panay* and the three nearby Standard Oil tankers. When the shelling resumed the next day, the gunboat's skipper, Lieutenant Commander James J. Hughes, decided to move the *Panay* farther upstream. Accompanied by the three Standard Oil tankers, the *Panay* dropped anchor about 25 miles upriver from Nanking. That afternoon, Japanese bombers struck the *Panay*. Within half an hour, the bombers had severely damaged the vessel, and the order was given to abandon her. Two launches carried the *Panay* crew ashore. Japanese planes then returned and strafed the gunboat with machine-gun fire sinking her and the three tankers. The *Panay* thus became the first American navy ship sunk by hostile aircraft. The survivors from the gunboat were picked up by a sister ship and reached Shanghai five days later. The United States government demanded an immediate apology and compensation for damages. Although the Japanese contended that the entire incident had been a mistake, an American photographer on board had taken pictures of Japanese planes attacking the *Panay*, whose American flags were clearly visible. The Japanese finally offered a com-

plete apology on Christmas Eve, and in April, 1938, presented a check for $2,214,007.36 for the death of the three Americans and the destruction of the *Panay* and the three tankers.

PERKINS, Frances (1882–1965). The first woman to be appointed to a Presidential cabinet, Miss Perkins served as Secretary of Labor from 1933 to 1945. Born in Boston, Miss Perkins graduated from Mount Holyoke College in 1902. She subsequently engaged in social work and teaching and re-

Secretary of Labor Frances Perkins went to Pittsburgh to talk with steelworkers.

ceived a Master's degree from Columbia University in 1910. As executive secretary of the New York Consumer's League from 1910 to 1912, Miss Perkins sought to improve working conditions for women and children and became an expert on industrial hazards and hygiene. After witnessing the tragic Triangle fire in a shirt factory in 1911, in which 146 employees died, she devoted the next several years to lobbying in New York State for safety legislation and maximum-hour laws for

women. Miss Perkins married Paul Caldwell Wilson in 1913 but continued to work under her maiden name. During the 1920s, she was appointed to various New York State industrial commissions by Governors Alfred E. Smith (1873–1944) and **Franklin D. Roosevelt** (*see*). After he became President in 1933, Roosevelt made Miss Perkins his Secretary of Labor. Although businessmen, labor leaders, and politicians denounced the appointment, and despite her failure to mediate disputes between the American Fed-

eration of Labor and the Committee for (later Congress of) Industrial Organizations, Miss Perkins ably administered her department with its vastly increased functions during the New Deal, and she kept the post until her retirement in 1945. From 1946 to 1952, she was a member of the Civil Service Commission.

POST, Wiley (1899–1935). Post was a well-known aviator who became the first man to fly around the world on his own. Born in

Texas, Post grew up in Oklahoma. Although uninterested in school as a child, he was fascinated by machines and took a brief course in an automobile school at the age of 17. He worked as a truck driver and then drilled oil in Oklahoma, before becoming a parachute jumper for some stunt pilots in 1924. Two years later, Post returned to the oil fields, where an accident cost him an eye. With money received in compensation for the injury, the aviator purchased a secondhand plane and gave flying exhibitions. In 1928, he was hired as a pilot by F. C. Hall, an Oklahoma oilman. Two years later, using Hall's plane, the *Winnie Mae,* Post won the Bendix Trophy Race from Los Angeles to Chicago. On June 23, 1931, Post and his navigator, Harold Gatty, took off in the *Winnie Mae* and flew 15,474 miles around the world in a record eight days, 15 hours, and 51 minutes (*see p. 1213*). Post himself piloted the plane the entire way. In 1933, he purchased the *Winnie Mae* from Hall and that July repeated the same flight alone, making the trip in seven days, 18 hours, and 49 minutes. The aviator subsequently became interested in high-altitude flight. He invented and tested a pressurized suit for use in the stratosphere. Through their common interest in flying, Post and the humorist Will Rogers (1879–1935) became friends. In 1935, the two men set out on a flight to the Orient by way of Siberia. Their plane crashed en route near Point Barrow, Alaska, killing both fliers.

R

ROBERTS, Owen Josephus (1875–1955). An Associate Justice of the Supreme Court from 1930 to 1945, Roberts was a central figure in many decisions involving the constitutionality of the New Deal

Owen J. Roberts

legislation of President **Franklin D. Roosevelt** (*see*). Like Chief Justice Charles Evans Hughes (1862–1948), he sided with neither the liberal nor the conservative wing of the Supreme Court, and his vote was frequently the crucial factor in Court rulings. Roberts received his undergraduate (1895) and law (1898) degrees from the University of Pennsylvania and then taught there (1898–1918) while practicing law in his native Philadelphia. From 1901 to 1904, he served as assistant district attorney of Philadelphia County. An outstanding trial lawyer, Roberts first gained national attention in 1924, when President Calvin Coolidge (1872–1933) named him a special federal prosecutor in the notorious Teapot Dome case, which involved the illegal leasing of naval oil reserves to private interests. Roberts' efforts helped to unearth the fraud and to secure the conviction of several of the conspirators. In 1930, Roberts was appointed to the Supreme Court by President Herbert Hoover (1874–1964). Although he had been a conservative Republican, Roberts soon became known for his independent judgment and un-

predictability. His vote invalidated the first Agricultural Adjustment Act in 1936, but he voted to uphold such radically innovative legislation as the Social Security Act and the Wagner Labor Relations Act in 1937. Roberts stood firm against Roosevelt's attempts to reorganize and dominate the Court (*see pp. 1253–1258*). However, just as the majority of the Justices did, he gradually moved toward a more sympathetic view of much of the New Deal program. In 1942, the President named Roberts chairman of a commission to investigate the Japanese attack on Pearl Harbor on December 7, 1941. Although the commission found the army commander, Lieutenant General Walter C. Short (1880–1949), and the navy commander, Rear Admiral Husband E. Kimmel (1882–1968), guilty of "dereliction of duty" and "errors of judgment" in being unprepared for the sneak attack, it recommended against court-martial proceedings. An outspoken opponent of isolationism and an advocate of world federalism, Roberts later added that America's smug "sense of superiority" was a contributing factor in the Pearl Harbor disaster. After retiring from the Supreme Court in 1945, Roberts served as dean of the University of Pennsylvania Law School (1948–1951). He wrote *The Court and the Constitution* in 1951.

ROBINSON, Joseph Taylor (1872–1937). As Senate majority leader from 1933 to 1937, Robinson directed the passage of many New Deal laws and led the fight for the unpopular Supreme Court reorganization bill of President **Franklin D. Roosevelt** (*see*). An Arkansas lawyer, Robinson served one term in the state legislature (1895–1897) before being elected to the United States House of Representatives (1903–1913). In

1912, Robinson was elected governor of Arkansas, but he resigned early the next year to fill out an unexpired term in the United States Senate. He remained a Senator for the rest of his life, becoming the Democratic floor leader in 1923. In 1928, Robinson was his party's Vice-Presidential nominee, running with Alfred E. Smith (1873–1944), who lost. As majority leader, Robinson supported Roosevelt on almost every New Deal measure. He was co-sponsor, with Representative Wright Patman (1893–1976) of Texas, of the Robinson-Patman Act (1936), an early fair-trade law. When the President attempted to reorganize the Supreme Court (*see pp. 1253–1258*), Robinson—although 65 years old—was offered the first available seat on the bench. In the midst of the debate on the reorganization bill, he died of a heart attack. The bill was subsequently shelved.

ROOSEVELT, (Anna) Eleanor (1884–1962). The wife of President **Franklin D. Roosevelt** (*see*), Eleanor Roosevelt was a humanitarian, diplomat, and controversial political personality in her own right. Her father, who was the younger brother of Theodore Roosevelt (1858–1919), died when Eleanor was 10, and the shy, homely girl was educated by private tutors. She then devoted herself to charity work. When she became engaged to Franklin Roosevelt, who was her fifth cousin, Eleanor was a volunteer inspector of women's lavatories in New York City's garment district. Over the objections of his domineering mother, Franklin married Eleanor in 1905, with President Theodore Roosevelt giving the bride away. Eleanor spent most of her time raising their six children, one of whom died in infancy (*see p. 1192*). When Franklin was stricken with polio in 1921, Eleanor rekindled his interest in politics and took on much of the

necessary leg work for her husband. She served as chairman of numerous women's committees and spoke in favor of youth movements, consumer welfare, and the rights of minorities. In 1933, she held the first press conference ever given by a President's wife. Two years later, Mrs. Roosevelt started a syndicated newspaper column, "My Day," describing her numerous projects—doling soup in a Depression line, visiting a WPA project, lunching with members of the railroad-porters union, reading to children in the Dust Bowl, or caring for the sick in the slums (*see p. 1198*). During World War II, she also served as assistant director of the Office of Civilian Defense and visited various battle fronts. When her husband died in 1945, Mrs. Roosevelt said, "My story is over." However, President Harry S. Truman (1884–1972) appointed her to the United States delegation to the United Nations, and she was elected chairman of the Commission on Human Rights. In that capacity, the "First Lady of the World" was instrumental in drafting the Declaration of Human Rights and in winning· the right to keep 1,000,000 refugees from being returned to Communist countries. Her books include *This I Remember* (1949), *On My Own* (1958), and *The Autobiography of Eleanor Roosevelt* (1961). Addressing the U.N. General Assembly at the time of her death, Ambassador Adlai E. Stevenson (1900–1965) said, "She would rather light candles than curse the darkness, and her glow warmed the world."

ROOSEVELT, Franklin Delano (1882–1945). As the 32nd President of the United States (1933–1945), Roosevelt—a tough, talented politician known for his charm and self-assurance—virtually remade the economic, political, and social fabric of America. His legislative achievements, col-

lectively called the New Deal, moved the nation toward increasing governmental intervention in the marketplace and a planned economy, thus extending Washington's influence into nearly every facet of national life. Roosevelt was born on the family estate at Hyde Park, New York (*see pp. 1187–1207*). Both his parents traced their ancestry to colonial times. After graduating from Harvard in 1904, Roosevelt studied law at Columbia University (1904–1907) and was admitted to the New York bar in 1907. During his second year at Columbia, he married a distant cousin, **Eleanor Roosevelt** (*see*), the niece of President Theodore Roosevelt (1858–1919). Roosevelt practiced law in New York for three years before he was elected to the state senate (1910–1913). After campaigning vigorously for the national Democratic ticket in 1912, he was named Assistant Secretary of the Navy (1913–1920) by President Woodrow Wilson (1856–1924) and was instrumental in strengthening the nation's naval power during World War I. In 1920, F.D.R.—as he was to become known to millions—was the Vice-Presidential candidate on the unsuccessful Democratic ticket headed by James M. Cox (1870–1957). The following summer, while vacationing in Canada on Campobello Island, off the coast of Maine, Roosevelt was stricken with polio, which left him paralyzed from the waist down. Encouraged by his wife, he gradually learned to walk again, with the aid of braces and crutches, but he was largely confined to a wheelchair for the rest of his life. Undaunted, he won election to the governorship of New York in 1928 and reelection two years later. Roosevelt's leadership in alleviating the hardships of the Depression in New York, his great personal magnetism, and his friendship with key Democratic leaders won him his party's Presidential nomination in 1932. He was swept into the White House by a landslide majority, winning 472 electoral votes to 59 for the incumbent Republican President, Herbert Hoover (1874–1964). An assassination attempt against the President-elect three weeks before his inauguration failed, but Chicago Mayor **Anton Cermak** (*see*) was killed in the assault (*see p. 1180*). Roosevelt began immediately to implement the "new deal" he had promised the nation. During his tumultuous first "Hundred Days" in office, the new President kept an anxious citizenry informed with a series of reassuring "fireside chats" over the radio. The day after he took office, Roosevelt declared a four-day national "bank holiday" to reassess the stability of financial institutions. Then, summoning Congress into a special session that lasted over three months and relying heavily on a corps of expert advisers known as his **Brain Trust** (*see*), Roosevelt pushed through Congress a revolutionary program of relief and reform legislation (*see pp. 1181–1186*). These so-called First New Deal programs were essentially emergency measures for coping with the Depression. Beginning in 1935, Roosevelt was more concerned with permanent social and labor reforms. This period—lasting until about 1939—is often termed the Second New Deal (*see pp. 1242–1244 and 1246–1251*). Growing opposition from conservative quarters was insufficient to prevent Roosevelt's smashing victory—523 electoral votes to 8 —over the Republican candidate, **Alfred M. Landon** (*see*), in the election of 1936. In 1937, F.D.R. tried to enlarge the Supreme Court, which for two years had been invalidating crucial New Deal measures (*see pp. 1253–1258*). His attempt to "pack" the Court with new Justices of more liberal persuasion was a failure, but the result was that the "Nine Old

UPI

Alabama militia guarded the Scottsboro Boys from lynchers before their 1931 trial.

Men" on the high tribunal suddenly became more receptive to the Roosevelt program. The pressing urgency of the nation's domestic problems did not cause Roosevelt to neglect foreign affairs. He established a "Good-Neighbor" policy toward Latin America, extended diplomatic recognition to the Communist regime in Russia in 1933, and continually warned the American people about the growing belligerence of Germany and Japan. After 1939, F.D.R. became increasingly absorbed with the worsening international situation. (*Entry continues in Volume 15.*)

ROSENMAN, Samuel. *See* **Brain Trust.**

SCOTTSBORO BOYS. On March 25, 1931, at Scottsboro, Alabama, two white girls, Ruby

Bates, 17, and Victoria Price, 21, falsely accused nine black youths of having raped them in the car of a moving freight train. These charges resulted in the so-called Scottsboro case, a series of sensational trials that lasted until 1937. During this period, the plight of the nine defandants, who came to be known as the Scottsboro Boys, became a *cause célèbre* among Northern liberals and radicals, who were outraged that Alabama juries ignored the conclusive evidence proving the boys' innocence. The boys, whose ages ranged from 13 to 20, were Olen Montgomery, Clarence Norris, Haywood Patterson, Ozie Powell, Willie Roberson, Charlie Weems, Eugene Williams, and two brothers, Andrew and Leroy Wright. At their first trial, which began 12 days after their arrest, the youths were defended by the Scottsboro Bar Association. An all-white jury sentenced all but Williams, who was only 13, to death. The International Labor Defense, a Communist organization, subsequently undertook their defense and appealed the verdict. The following March, the Alabama supreme court upheld the verdict but excluded Leroy Wright, who was also a minor, from the death sentence. The case was then appealed to the United States Supreme Court, which in November, 1932, granted a retrial on the ground that the defendants had not been given adequate counsel. The Court cited the Fourteenth Amendment, which prohibits any state from depriving "any person of life, liberty, or property, without due process of law." In two further trials in Alabama courts in March and December, 1933, two of the boys were sentenced to death, in spite of the fact that Ruby Bates recanted her story. She now testified that neither she nor Victoria Price had been raped. The case was again appealed to the Supreme Court. In April, 1935, the Court ruled in favor of the Scottsboro Boys on the ground that blacks had been systematically excluded from all the juries that had tried them. The following November, a Scottsboro grand jury that included one black indicted the nine on the charge of rape. In January, 1936, an all-white jury convicted Patterson, this time sentencing him to 75 years in prison. At the final trial in July, 1937, Norris was sentenced to death; Andrew Wright and Weems were given long prison terms; Powell, who pleaded guilty to the knife assault of a deputy sheriff, was given 20 years; and the remaining four were freed. All those who were imprisoned were eventually freed or paroled except for Patterson, who briefly escaped in 1948. He died of cancer in another prison four years later. Andrew Wright, who was granted a parole in 1950, was the last to be freed. "Everywhere I go," he said later, "it seems like Scottsboro is

Stimson stumped New York State in his unsuccessful bid to be governor in 1910.

throwed up in my face. I don't believe I'll ever live it down." Ruby Bates and Victoria Price both died in 1961.

SECOND NEW DEAL. *See* **Roosevelt, Franklin D.**

STIMSON, Henry Lewis (1867–1950). A respected statesman and diplomat, Stimson served in the cabinets of four Presidents. Born in New York, he graduated from Harvard Law School in 1890 and practiced law in New York City until he was appointed a federal district attorney in 1906. Four years later, Stimson ran as the Republican candidate for governor of New York but was defeated. In 1911, President William Howard Taft (1857–1930) appointed Stimson his Secretary of War. He served until Taft left office two years later. He resumed his law practice in New York, but at the age of 49, enlisted in the army and fought in the last campaigns of World War I in France. From 1927 to 1929, Stimson was governor-general of the Philippines. President Herbert Hoover (1874–1964) appointed him Secretary of State in 1929. In that post, Stimson led the United States

delegations to the London Naval Conference in 1930 and to the 1931 Disarmament Conference in Geneva. When the Japanese invaded Manchuria in 1931, Stimson suggested that America respond with force or a threat of force. Hoover vetoed the idea. Instead, the United States' reaction was confined to the so-called Stimson Doctrine. This doctrine, which Stimson based on the Kellogg-Briand Pact outlawing war, advocated nonrecognition of territories gained by war. Stimson again returned to his law practice in 1933. When President **Franklin D. Roosevelt** (*see*) named him Secretary of War in July, 1940, the Republican Party drummed Stimson out of its ranks for accepting the post. He remained in the cabinet under President Harry S. Truman (1884–1972) until the end of World War II. Stimson, who had briefed Truman on the potentialities of the atomic bomb, published his autobiography, *On Active Service in Peace and War*, in 1948.

STONE, Harlan Fiske (1872–1946). As both an Associate Justice of the United States Supreme Court (1925–1941) and then the

Chief Justice (1941–1946), Stone was one of the important jurists of the New Deal era. He joined Justices Oliver Wendell Holmes (1841–1935) and **Louis D. Brandeis** (*see*) as a "great dissenter," consistently supporting the constitutionality of New Deal legislation against the conservative majority on the Court during the 1930s. A native of Chesterfield, New Hampshire, Stone graduated from Amherst College in 1894 and from the Columbia University Law School in 1898. While practicing law in New York City, he served on the Columbia law faculty from 1899 to 1923, holding the post of dean after 1910. Appointed Attorney General of the United States by President Calvin Coolidge (1872–1933) in 1924, Stone reorganized the Federal Bureau of Investigation and helped restore public confidence in the Justice Department after notorious governmental corruption of the early 1920s. Stone was named to the Supreme Court by Coolidge in 1925. Originally a conservative Republican, he surprised many people by arguing

Harlan F. Stone

for the constitutionality of most of the legislative program of President **Franklin D. Roosevelt** (*see*), including such controversial measures as the Agricultural Adjustment Act. One of Stone's memorable dissents came in what was known as the Jehovah's Witnesses' case (1940), when he held that state governments could not compel citizens to salute the flag if this conflicted with their religion. This view was later adopted by

the Court in 1943. Elevated to Chief Justice by Roosevelt in 1941, Stone summarized his legal philosophy in stating that law is a "human institution for human needs . . . not an end but a means to an end." He suffered a fatal stroke while reading a dissenting opinion against prohibiting citizenship to an immigrant who refused to bear arms.

SUNDAY, William Ashley ("Billy") (1862–1935). A flamboyant evangelist who toured the United States for more than 30 years urging spiritual laggards to "Get right with God," Billy Sunday persuaded hundreds of thousands of people to make a religious "decision." The high point of his popularity came in 1910, when his well-organized meetings attracted huge throngs and furnished Billy with a substantial fortune from "freewill offerings." Combining a zeal for conversions with a theatrical flair, Sunday deplored Christians who were "hog-jowled, weasel-eyed, sponge-columned, mushy-fisted, jelly-spined, pussy-footing, four-flush-

Baseball-player-turned-evangelist, Billy Sunday minced no words in urging sinners to "Get right with God."

ing, charlotte-ruse." Sunday, whose father, a Civil War soldier, died shortly after the boy's birth, was reared in orphanages in his native Iowa. Beginning about 1876, he worked at numerous odd jobs as a farmhand, janitor, undertaker's helper, and store clerk in various Iowa towns. While playing baseball at Marshalltown in 1883, Sunday was spotted by Adrian C. "Cap" Anson (1852–1922), captain of the Chicago White Stockings, who signed him to a major-league contract. Sunday—"good field, no hit"—played the outfield for the White Sox from 1883 to 1888 and then spent three years with teams in Pittsburgh and Philadelphia. After leaving baseball in 1891, Billy, who had experienced a religious conversion in 1887, worked for the Chicago Y. M. C. A. for several years. In 1898, he was licensed as a preacher and began making religious converts. A staunch opponent of strong drink, Billy helped pave the way for the Eighteenth Amendment that established prohibition in 1920. He once called a drunken member of his audience a "dirty, low-down, whisky-soaked, beer-guzzling, bull-necked, foul-mouthed hypocrite!" Sunday often made use of imagery drawn from his baseball days, exhorting his hearers to "Take a stand and get into the game!" and bemoaning the fact that "there are a lot of people who step up to the collection plate and fan." After World War I, Sunday's homespun sermons and fire-and-brimstone revivals declined sharply in popularity, and he died in relative obscurity. His publications include *Burning Truths from Billy's Bat* (1914) and *Seventy-four Complete Sermons of the Omaha Campaign* (1915).

SUTHERLAND, George (1862–1942).

One of the "Nine Old Men" on the United States Supreme Court, Sutherland staunchly opposed President **Franklin D. Roosevelt** (*see*) in his attempt to reorganize the Court (*see pp. 1253–1258*). British by birth, Sutherland came to America with his parents in 1864. After studying law at the University of Michigan, he established a practice in Utah in 1883. A Republican, Sutherland served in the state legislature from 1896 to 1900. He later held seats in the House of Representatives (1901–1903) and the Senate (1905–1917). Appointed an Associate Justice of the Supreme Court in 1922, the jurist established a reputation for handing down conservative opinions. He aligned himself with Justices **Willis Van Devanter, Pierce Butler,** and **James C. McReynolds** (*see all*) in opposing many New Deal measures. In 1938, a year after Roosevelt attempted to reorganize the Court, Sutherland retired at the age of 76.

T

TOWNSEND, Francis Everett (1867–1960).

A physician by profession, Townsend was the leader of an old-age pension movement during the Depression. Born in Illinois, he graduated from the Omaha Medical College at the University of Nebraska in 1903 and practiced in several Western states before settling in Long Beach, California, in 1919. Townsend organized Old-Age Revolving Pensions, Inc. in 1933 to put into effect a program that was popularly called the Townsend Plan. It called for a pension of $200 a month to be given to any person over 60 years of age if the pensioner was unemployed and spent the entire sum in the United States within 30 days of receiving it. The plan, which was to be financed by a 2% federal sales tax, was designed both to provide for the elderly and to stimulate the nation's depressed economy. Of the many "share-the-wealth" plans

Francis E. Townsend

conceived during the Depression, the Townsend Plan was one of the most popular, even though it was criticized by many economists. Townsend Clubs were organized all over the nation, and the movement's periodical, *The Townsend National Weekly,* enjoyed a circulation of more than 200,000 copies. At the height of its popularity, Old-Age Revolving Pensions, Inc. had 2,500,000 members and about 10 times that many supporters. However, Congress defeated all legislation for the adoption of the plan. The movement's strength began to decline after the passage of the Social Security Act of 1935—which established, among other provisions, a national old-age insurance —and with the gradual recovery of the nation's economy. By 1941, the Townsend Plan had lost most of its support. Townsend published his autobiography, *New Horizons,* in 1943.

TUGWELL, Rexford G. *See* Brain Trust.

TWENTIETH AMENDMENT.

This amendment, called the lame-duck amendment, changed the date of the annual opening of Congress from March 4 to January 3 and thereby eliminated the so-called lame-duck session of Congress—the period from December to March—in which members who had failed to win reelection in the previous Congressional elections still had the power to pass laws. Ratified in February, 1933, and effective as of the following October, the Twentieth Amendment also established January 20 as the date for the inauguration of the President. Previously, Presidents had begun their terms of office on March 4. Other provisions of the amendment set forth the procedures for choosing a President under special circumstances, such as the death of the President-elect before the beginning of his term of office. In such a situation, the Vice-President-elect becomes President. If neither the President- nor the Vice-President-elect "qualify" for the Presidency, then the choice of either or both of these officers was left to Congress. Congress, which was responsible for framing the Twentieth Amendment, made no attempt to interpret what the word "qualify" meant. In 1967, the Twenty-fifth Amendment was ratified to provide for the line of Presidential succession in case of disability.

TWENTY-FIRST AMENDMENT. This amendment, which went into effect immediately after its ratification in December, 1933, repealed the Eighteenth Amendment, which had established prohibition almost 14 years earlier. Prohibition had been a catastrophic failure. Instead of improving American morality, it contributed to illicit liquor traffic and the general lawlessness of the Roaring Twenties. Gangland racketeers prospered through their control of liquor, and bootleggers sold bottles of alcoholic beverages for high prices. During the "wet" years prior to 1919, there were about 15,000 saloons in the United

States. During prohibition, these were replaced by nearly 32,000 speakeasies, usually run by gangster syndicates. The notorious gangster **Al Capone** (*see*) actually received fan mail applauding his brazen disregard for prohibition. By the late 1920s, politicians regularly included the prohibition issue in their platforms. In 1929, when it was obvious that the federal government's inability to enforce the Eighteenth Amendment was creating serious social problems, President Herbert Hoover (1874–1964), who had called prohibition the Noble Experiment, appointed a law observance and enforcement commission to study the Eighteenth Amendment. Known as the Wickersham Commission after its chairman, former Attorney General George W. Wickersham (1858–1936), it reported in 1931 that prohibition was virtually unenforceable. Nevertheless, the commission was opposed to the repeal of the amendment. Public opinion, however, was strongly in favor of repeal, especially after the stock-market crash of 1929 (*see* **Black Tuesday**), when federal and state governments needed every penny they could get, including revenue from liquor taxes. When **Franklin D. Roosevelt** (*see*) accepted the Democratic Party's Presidential nomination in 1932, he announced that "from this day on, the Eighteenth Amendment is doomed." The Twenty-first Amendment was proposed in February, 1933, and was ratified by the necessary 36 states within 10 months.

TYDINGS, Millard Evelyn (1890–1961). A Democratic Senator from Maryland (1927–1951), Tydings first won national prominence during the 1938 Congressional elections, when President **Franklin D. Roosevelt** (*see*) tried to "purge" him because he had opposed his attempt to reorganize the Supreme Court in 1937 (*see pp.*

DYNAMITE.

Prohibition was a touchy issue as late as 1931, two years before its repeal.

1253–1258). The Senator was victorious and returned to the Senate, only to be unseated 12 years later after denouncing Senator Joseph R. McCarthy (1909–1957) of Wisconsin, who claimed that the State Department was "infested" with Communists. Born in Maryland, Tydings received a law degree from the University of Maryland in 1913. That year, he set up what soon became a flourishing law practice, and three years later he was elected to the state legislature. In 1917, on the eve of America's entry into World War I, Tydings enlisted in the army as a private. He served in France and Germany and by the end of the war was a lieutenant colonel with a Distinguished Service Medal and the Distinguished Service Cross. Tydings served in the Maryland senate (1921–1923) and the House of Representatives (1923–1927) before entering the Senate in 1927. His conservatism and belief in states' rights led him to oppose many of Roosevelt's New Deal measures in the 1930s. Despite the President's opposition, he received a record vote when he campaigned for reelection in the Maryland Senatorial

Millard E. Tydings

primary of 1938. In February, 1950, Tydings was appointed chairman of a special Senate foreign-relations subcommittee set up to examine McCarthy's charges of communism in the State Department. The following July, he reported that McCarthy's assertions were untrue and "contemptible." That fall, after an extremely bitter race, in which McCarthy sympathizers circulated a doctored photograph showing Tydings talking to Communist Party leader Earl Browder (1891–1973), Tydings lost his Senate seat. He was nominated for the Senate again in 1956 but withdrew from the contest because of illness. He subsequently practiced law in Washington, D.C. His stepson, Joseph D. Tydings (born 1928), was elected to the Senate in 1964.

V

VANDENBERG, Arthur Hendrick (1884–1951). A Republican Senator for 23 years, Vandenberg reversed his pre-World War II isolationist position to become a leading internationalist in Congress and a champion of a bipartisan foreign policy. His support was invaluable in establishing the United Nations, the Marshall Plan, and the North Atlantic Treaty Organization. Vandenberg was the editor of the Grand Rapids (Michigan) *Herald* when he was appointed to fill a Senate vacancy in 1928. He was subsequently elected to four terms and by 1937 was considered the leader of Senate Republicans. In 1936, 1940, and 1948, Vandenberg received some support for the Republican Presidential nomination. Prior to the Japanese attack on Pearl Harbor on December 7, 1941, Vandenberg opposed Lend-Lease aid to Britain and all other proposals that would involve the United States in the war. After the attack, however—which, he said, "ended isolationism for any realist"—he gave full support to the

Arthur H. Vandenberg

administration's war effort. Vandenberg served on the Senate "Committee of Eight," which was charged with formulating postwar plans, and by the end of the war he was the leading Republican spokesman on international affairs. In a Senate speech in January, 1945, Vandenberg renounced his isolationism and indicated he would not oppose membership in the United Nations. President **Franklin D. Roosevelt** (*see*) appointed him a delegate to the charter conference of the United Nations in San Francisco, and in December, 1945, President Harry S. Truman (1884–1972) named him a delegate to the U.N. General Assembly. As chairman of the Senate Foreign Relations Committee (1947–1949), Vandenberg supported the Truman Doctrine, under which the United States aided Greece and Turkey against Communist aggression. He also was instrumental in securing passage of the European Recovery Act, or Marshall Plan. Vandenberg introduced in the Senate a resolution committing the United States to "collective self-defense." This became the basis for American participation in the North Atlantic Treaty Organization.

VAN DEVANTER, Willis (1859–1941). As an Associate Justice of the Supreme Court (1910–1937), Van Devanter was—along with Justices **Pierce Butler, James C. McReynolds,** and **George Sutherland** (*see all*)—one of the four conservatives who opposed nearly every New Deal measure advocated by President **Franklin D. Roosevelt** (*see*) in the 1930s. His retirement in May, 1937, came in the midst of the President's unsuccessful attempt to enlarge the Court (*see pp. 1253–1258*). Born in Indiana, Van Devanter graduated from Cincinnati Law School in 1881. He practiced in Indiana for the next three years and then moved to Cheyenne, Wyoming, where he set up a legal practice and later served as city attorney (1887–1888). After a year (1889–1890) as chief justice of the Wyoming supreme court, Van Devanter worked as counsel for some of the most powerful business interests in the state, including the Union Pacific Railroad. He also became prominent in Republican politics, first as the chairman of the party's state committee (1892–1894) and later as a national committeeman (1896–1900). Van Devanter campaigned for William McKinley (1843–1901) in 1896 and was rewarded the following year with a cabinet appointment as Assistant Attorney General. He resigned that office in 1903 to become a United States circuit court judge, a position he retained until President William Howard Taft (1857–1930) appointed him to the Supreme Court in 1910. As a Justice, Van Devanter was known for his strict interpretation of the Constitution and the priority he gave to big-business interests. After Van Devanter retired from the Supreme Court, he served for a year (1938) as a federal district judge in New York City.

W

WALLACE, Henry Agard (1888–1965). Wallace was a central figure in the New Deal administration of President **Franklin D. Roosevelt** (*see*), serving as Secretary of Agriculture from 1933 to 1940 and as Vice-President between 1941 and 1945 (*see p. 1240*). He was appointed Secretary of Commerce in 1945 but was asked to resign

the next year for criticizing the foreign policy of Roosevelt's successor, Harry S. Truman (1884–1972). Wallace then helped organize the Progressive Party and polled more than 1,000,000 votes as the party's Presidential candidate in 1948. Wallace was born in Adair County, Iowa, the son of Henry C. Wallace (1866–1924) and the grandson of Henry Wallace (1836–1916), cofounders of *Wallaces' Farmer,* the nation's leading farm journal of the period. Henry C. Wallace was Secretary of Agriculture (1921–1924) under Presidents Warren G. Harding (1865–1923) and Calvin Coolidge (1872–1933). After graduating from Iowa State College in 1910, young Wallace joined the staff of the family journal, serving as associate editor (1910–1924) and then as editor (1924–1933). He also conducted experiments in plant genetics and developed several strains of hybrid corn used widely in the Midwest. His reputation as an expert on agrarian problems and his support of Roosevelt in 1932 led the new President to appoint Wallace—who once said his goal was "to make the world safe for corn-breeders"

—to head the Department of Agriculture. Wallace reorganized the department, and as the head also of the Agricultural Adjustment Administration, worked to stabilize the nation's food production by encouraging more diversified farming, giving subsidies to farmers, and instituting crop-production controls. While Vice-President, Wallace also directed the Board of Economic Warfare. His diplomatic skill was a factor in bettering relations with several Latin-American and Asian nations. Despite the fact that many believed Wallace to be Roosevelt's "heir apparent," he was brushed aside at the urging of conservative Democrats in favor of Truman as the party's Vice-Presidential candidate in 1944. Wallace's brief term in the Truman cabinet ended abruptly in 1946 after he publicly took issue with the President's "get-tough" stand toward Russia. Wallace, the last of the original New Dealers to leave office, then served as editor of the liberal *New Republic* (1946–1947). Advocating the easing of East-West tensions and opposing universal military training, Wallace announced his third-party candidacy for President in late 1947, after denouncing the "dry rot" in the major parties. However, the Progressive Party was viewed with suspicion by many voters because of the strong influence of radical leftists, and he polled less than 3% of the vote in the 1948 election, which was won by Truman. In 1950, having parted company with the Progressives over the Korean War issue, Wallace retired to a farm in New York State. His writings, in addition to many books on agricultural matters, include *Paths to Plenty* (1938), *The Century of the Common Man* (1943), *Toward World Peace* (1948), and *The Long Look Ahead* (1960).

WHITE, William Allen (1868–1944). One of the most noted

Despite heckling, Progressive Henry Wallace tried to woo Southern voters in 1948.

William Allen White

journalists in American history, White was the editor and publisher of the *Gazette* in his home town, Emporia, Kansas, for nearly half a century. White had attended two colleges without graduating from either. He worked on a number of state newspapers, including the Kansas City *Star,* before purchasing the Emporia *Gazette* in 1895. White gained national attention during the Presidential campaign the following year when he printed his famous editorial "What's the Matter with Kansas?" In it, he criticized the free-silver position of the Democratic Party candidate, William Jennings Bryan (1860–1925), and condemned the people of Kansas—most of whom were supporting Bryan—for their desire for "money power." This editorial, which was reprinted throughout the nation, helped put

the Republican candidate, William McKinley (1843–1901), in the White House. White's editorials reflected the ideals of the middle-class, small-town Republicans of the Middle West. However, he did not always write about politics. One of his most widely read articles was his tribute to his daughter, Mary, who died in 1921 at the age of 17. The following year, he was awarded a Pulitzer Prize for his editorial "To an Anxious Friend," which was a sympathetic discussion of a railroad-workers' strike. The most important collections of White's newspaper writings are *The Editor and His People* (1924) and *Forty Years on Main Street* (1937). The best examples of his fiction are *In Our Town* (1906), a collection of short stories, and *A Certain Rich Man* (1909), a novel set in post-Civil War Kansas. White also wrote *Woodrow Wilson: The Man, The Times, and His Task* (1924), *Calvin Coolidge, the Man Who is President* (1925), and *A Puritan in Babylon: The Story of Calvin Coolidge* (1938). White's *Autobiography* (1946) and *Selected Letters* (1947) were published after his death.

WOOD, Grant (1891–1942). This famous American artist was known for his realistic paintings of the rural Midwest. Born in Iowa, Wood studied at the Minneapolis School of Design and Handicraft and later at the Art Institute of Chi-

Grant Wood

cago. He then continued his studies at the Academie Julian in Paris. In 1927, Wood was commissioned to execute a stained-glass window for the Memorial Building in Cedar Rapids, Iowa. To employ the skilled craftsmen necessary for the project, he traveled to Germany the following year. There Wood was impressed by the work of the 15th- and 16th-century German and Flemish painters. At the same time, he was influenced by the German realist painters of the 19th and 20th centuries. After his return to the United States, Wood began painting realistic, formalized scenes of the countryside in which he had grown up. His most famous work, *American Gothic,* a stark portrait of a Midwestern farmer and his daughter (*see p. 1227*), was painted in 1930. It was followed by *Victorian Survival* (1931), *Daughters of Revolution* (1932), and *Parson Weems' Fable* (1939)—all of which served to rank Wood with **Thomas Hart Benton** (*see*) as the best-known American-scene painters of their day. During the Depression, Wood directed the Public Works of Art Project in Iowa.

WRIGHT, Frank Lloyd (1869–1959). By using new methods of construction and new materials and applying the philosophy that form must follow function, Wright revolutionized architectural design throughout the world. Born in Richland Center, Wisconsin, Wright entered the University of Wisconsin in 1884 to study civil engineering. Four years later, he moved to Chicago and began a six-year apprenticeship under the foremost architects of the day, including Louis H. Sullivan (1856–1924). After 1894, Wright operated out of his own architectural office in Oak Park, Illinois. From the beginning, Wright departed from the cluttered "gingerbread" style of Victorian architecture. Instead, he produced designs that were

Architect Frank Lloyd Wright's unique Guggenheim Museum in New York City was completed the year he died.

striking in their originality and simplicity. Typical was the Larkin Administration Building, built in Buffalo, New York, in 1904 (no longer standing). The building, the first to have air conditioning, established Wright's reputation nationally. During the early years of the 20th century, Wright perfected his "prairie" style, which emphasized long, low lines and sharply projecting eaves that harmonized with the flat Midwestern surroundings. This style also featured large windows, open terraces, and unified interior spaces in which walls between rooms were often eliminated. Two examples of this style, both situated in the vicinity of Chicago, include the Heurtley House (1902) in Oak Park and the Frederick C. Robie House (1909) at the University of Chicago. Wright's own residence in Spring Green, Wisconsin,

"Taliesin,"—built in 1911 and rebuilt twice after fires—was a forerunner of the modern ranch house. During the 1920s, his pupils lived a communal existence there, while studying with him. After 1910, Wright began substituting external ornamentation for simple surfaces, as seen in the Imperial Hotel (1916–1922) in Tokyo, Japan. The hotel was also distinctive for its "floating" foundation, which enabled it to withstand the earthquake of 1923 that leveled Tokyo's other major buildings. In the 1920s, Wright was one of the first architects to employ patterned blocks of precast concrete. These gave his structures a severe appearance and have since become standard in a majority of office and apartment buildings. After 1930, Wright was preoccupied with creating architectural effects through the distribution of masses

or shapes and the use of modern materials. Examples of this technique are the Johnson Wax Administration Building (1936–1939) in Racine, Wisconsin; "Taliesin West" (1936–1959), near Phoenix, Arizona; and "Falling Water" (1936–1937), a house cantilevered over a waterfall in Bear Run, Pennsylvania. Following World War II, Wright's major innovations were the dynamic interior spaces and spiral ramps of the Solomon R. Guggenheim Museum (1956–1959) in New York City. At his death, Wright left several unrealized projects, including one for a mile-high skyscraper in Chicago.

Z

ZANGARA, Giuseppe. *See* **Cermak, Anton.**